BUSINESS INSIDER with a TEENAGER

Shirley Martin Wang

Business Insider with a Teenager © Copyright <<2020>> Shirley Martin Wang
Copyright Notice: All rights reserved.
No part of this publication may be reproduced, distributed or transmitted in any form or by any means, including photocopying, recording, or other electronic or mechanical methods, without the prior written permission of the author, except in the case of brief quotations embodied in critical reviews and certain other noncommercial uses permitted by copyright law. For more information, email shirleytbusiness@gmail.com

To every teenager

who is willing to dream big, work hard,

and achieve something much greater than themselves...

Contents

Prologue

    Advice from an unqualified business author.

1 Getting Down To Business

    I am a young and aspiring businessman or businesswoman...

    but how do I start a business?

2 Let's Work (Il)legally!

    I am a teenager and I want to start working, but how can I do so legally?

3 Teenage Entrepreneur Stories

    I have seen other teenagers that have launched their own successful businesses... but how did they do it?

4 People, People, People

    I am currently a student...

    but how can school prepare me for my future career?

5 Social Media + Gen Z

    I am an Instagram, YouTube, Twitter, Pinterest, TikTok, or SnapChat user,

    but how do you make money off social media?

6 How To Pitch Yourself

    I interviewed for a job today, but why didn't I GET the job?

7 Smash The System

    I am sick of wearing suits and sticking to the old-fashioned rules,

    so how do I break the system?

8 Stereotyping

    I'm constantly getting rejected by employers because of my age, how do I change that?

Afternote

Just one last thing.

Acknowledgments

About The Author

Prologue

Advice from an unqualified business author.

Starting a business under the legal age of 18 is, without a doubt, a difficult feat.

If you picked up this book today, it could mean a variety of things: A) you want to make money, B) you have a profitable idea that you want to try out, or C) you realize that five-year-olds are making millions off their YouTube channel and you want to do the same. But surprise! Success does not run down the pipes. To be in the business industry and compete against the toughest individuals in the game, it will take much more than picking up this book and having a dream.

Instead of convincing you that I am the CEO of some multimillion-dollar corporation or whatever story you want to hear, I won't be living up to society's antiquated and outdated expectations. This is a book for teenagers – a generation that deserves to design an entire epoch for themselves without the burden of traditional ideology.

I grew up with the expectation to know my place, and if I stepped out of society's categorical boxes, there would be consequences without question. I grew up with certain adults in my life constantly making me feel less knowledgeable, less educated, less experienced. In their "logical" opinion, I did not deserve the right to have any opinion due to my age, so I learned to keep my mouth shut.

Is age-shaming an official thing? I don't know.

So, I am breaking the rules and the stereotypes. I am writing a business book as someone with a LACK of business experience, but a hell lot of advice for TEENAGERS that want to make money, start their own business, and growing beyond their school borders.

Instead of scrapping for internships, trying to get in contact with thousands of entrepreneurs via social media for business advice, or watching countless hours of YouTube to learn how to do something as basic as apply for a job, my book has bundled that all up. I've done the work, and now you get to reap the benefits.

This is not the conventional Steve Jobs or Mark Zuckerberg book that belongs on a shelf with all the business gurus and the stories of their many business ventures.

Business Insider with a Teenager is specifically designed for teenagers and their problems. You have the minimum age of employment to dodge, the 'lack of experience' written across your CV, and your age to give you another damn problem to overcome.

So – you can see that the situation is quite different.

1
Getting Down To Business

I am a young and aspiring businessman or businesswoman… but how do I start a business?

1. Dwell In Your Passions

You are constantly being bombarded with question about your passions, and what you want to be in the future.

At age 5, you might have wanted to become a pilot. At 10, you wanted to build Legos for a living. At 15, you want to shut your senile parents out of your bedroom and check your DMs from your friends before you go to bed. High school may seem too early a time to pen down your future, or to dedicate your life to one career route. You're thinking about experiences, places to go, celebrities you want to meet, and everything that you could possibly want from this world. In the back of your mind, you have a handful of passions that you mingle with from time to time, but you're not absolutely certain about ONE of them.

To begin this chapter, I want to reiterate the fact that high school is a period of experience. On the other hand, if you dabble in five different passions a year and never succeed in creating something more out of those passions… you've gathered knowledge on scattered topics and you've basically wasted your own time. Many people surf from one interest to the next, but the process won't get you anywhere.

My first lesson to you is to find ONE passion. And stick with it.

How Can You Stick With Your Passion?

After you find ONE passion, practice it over and over again. Execute it till you reach perfection. When you reach perfection, set a higher standard for yourself (something that exceeds the norms of "perfection"), and attain those new goals. When you attain those goals, contemplate your next step. Ask yourself what you can do to achieve higher or do better.

You can compare/contrast yourself to professionals in the industry, and study how they have walked their path to success. Analyze their pattern to success and learn from it.

You also can challenge other people in the industry who have achieved more than you; through this method, you can easily pinpoint your weakness and begin to strengthen them immediately. This is so you can follow your personalized version of their path to your own goals.

A third method is to surround yourself with people willing to critique you, motivate you, and constantly push you to do better. To conclude, hone your passion and creative juices into work, work, work.

2. Don't Jump The Ship

As we discuss the topic of honing your passion, your question of "how can I strive towards a future of success with this passion" comes into play.

One of the main make-or-break points of your career is how easily you give up.

Here is one obvious truth. Normal people give up. Successful people don't recognize the phrase "give up" in their dictionary. This is the simple yet exquisite silver lining between the mediocrity of the majority and the success of the few.

Your ability to stay determined and not give up is a measurement of your success in everyday life as well as business. Take this simple scenario as an example... A household member asks you to get milk, eggs, and a jug of water from the grocery store.

In scenario A, you only buy the milk and the eggs, because my excuses are that you either forgot to bring enough money to pay for all three items or your hands could not carry all three items back to the house.

Not only is the task left incomplete, it is masked by excuses. The excuses create holes in your reputation, and the shaping of your character. Because you faced the easy task with excuses and weak determination, it is unlikely that you will be asked to do it again. Success is not a matter of excuses.

In business, if you fail at the most minimalistic tasks, you are likely to fail at executing larger projects.

In scenario B, you buy all three items as requested. In the following weeks, you will gain the trust of your family, who will continue trusting you with more tasks in the future. Having consistent achievements and commitments is an essential habit to build you your future.

Creating a business relies on consistency, and the quality of your product/service. But thriving in the business world requires you to take that next step, make upgrades, and change your product/service to fit what the world needs:

In scenario C, you check the refrigerator and review what items we have and don't have. You inquire the household cook on the specific meals that they are planning on making for the following week and take note on the ingredients needed. When you come back from the grocery store, not only have you bought the milk, eggs, and jug of water, but you have also bought all the groceries for the week.

When the analogy is translated into business terms, you might be an employee… and there is a possibility that you might get in trouble for doing something wrong or getting the wrong items by taking a further step.

At the time, many of the other employees stay in their comfort zones and accomplish scenario B while you have taken the next step to impress your boss by analyzing what is needed and accomplishing more to fill in the potentially problematic gaps. This skill of understanding the necessity of taking risks and being smart about the risks is the key to your jumpstart at success.

Something that most people don't recognize is that taking risks is a fundamental and exciting part of the business industry. As teenagers, excitement, anticipation, and reward fuels creativity and the becoming of new ideas. If you are constantly in an industry where you are taking the right risks and you are not 100% sure if you can hit your goal every time, it creates a certain suspense that will make you want to do it all again… This business adrenaline can ensure that you keep coming back to hone your craft, work on your ideas, and make your business even better.

One Sentence Recap

Making no excuses, maintaining consistency, and taking risks are the three factors that will ensure that you never give up doing what you are passionate about through a business perspective.

3. Create A ~ Unique ~ Product/Service

Now, let's get down to business. It's time to fixate your passion into profit.

There are a lot of aspects that contribute to the creation of a product or service, which is the centerpiece of your business. So, how do entrepreneurs decide what their product or service should be?

As you look through the products and services that could be created from your passion, ask yourself the following questions to see which ones are best for your market.

A) What is the world lacking?

Business ideas are often born right after the phrase "why hasn't anyone thought about creating _____ ?"

With the help of AI and technology, people are seeking to spend more time doing the things that they enjoy instead of having to spend hours with house chores or repetitive jobs. What the world lacks becomes the perfect business opportunity for you, because you can invent or create something that will make people's lives easier and fill in the gap for something that other people in the same industry have yet to offer.

B) What do people want and/or need?

In the process of creating your product or outlining your service, put yourself in the shoes of your consumer. Why would they want to buy your product/service, if your competitor sold a similar one for a cheaper price? What is so special or unique about your product/service that you won't find anywhere else? Why will people buy this product/service from YOU? Once you narrow down your product or service, you can begin writing a formal business proposal to potential investors or collaborators.

4. The Thing With Investors

You're underage, unemployed, and you also want to start a business. This puts you in a unique situation that can be as advantageous as it is disadvantageous. Without a salary or a good amount of money to launch a startup, most entrepreneurs turn to the bank for a loan. In the special case of teenage entrepreneurs, you can either talk to your parents, friends, other family members, adult figures, or anyone you know that you can trust to give you a loan for the startup, or go old-fashion and ask a bank for a loan or contact possible investors.

However, the actual process of making someone hand you a big fat check isn't as easy as it sounds.

To begin with, you have to offer a well-constructed argument. Business proposals are meant to convince and persuade buyers or investors to bet their money on you. Smart entrepreneurs and businesspeople are not irrational decision makers. On the bright side, you are most likely to convince a person that you are familiar with to invest in your business. So, what does a business proposal look like?

Considering that you might be under 18, which may lower your credibility to adult investors, argue your way out of the 'disadvantages' side of the spectrum.

1

Watch Out For The Watering Hole

If you've been sitting under a rock, it's high time that I reveal to you that every business industry has its own foul play. Competition is what drives innovation and quality of product, which evidently produces some people that want your money above all else.

Let's say that you're beginning to share your business plan, and it's a genius idea. Someone can easily steal this idea from you, since — hell — there isn't any copyright. This is where you have to be especially careful to who you are talking to and who you are sharing your information with.

Discuss your business plan with possible investors that you trust, but don't go obliviously contacting unknown people on LinkedIn asking advice on your business idea after you've explained and revealed every last detail.

This is especially relevant to us teenage entrepreneurs, because we are perceived as an innocent teenager trying to break into industry. If someone you don't quite know offers you a deal or an investment, take some time to consider their proposal. Understand their background, talk to people that this individual has worked with in the past, and analyze how this person manages business situations. Deciding your investors can be a tedious process but finding the right ones can help support you and your business in the long run. Be SMART about who to trust and who not to trust.

2
Be Confident

Before you deliver your big speech, be prepared for a bit of an interrogation or some tough questions. You can expect a misconception of your business's purpose or questioning of your ability to run a full-on business being both underaged and unexperienced. Firstly, if you are trying to convince investors, there will be concerns of your age. Answer every question with your utmost confidence and assurance. When it comes to assuring your investors, convince them that you are able to handle the amount of workload that comes with a startup. Assure investors that you will be able to balance your schoolwork with the startup launch work.

Secondly, the businesspeople or experienced individuals in your family might try to talk you out of this with stories of their difficult path to launching a business. In spite of any concern or criticism, it is important to keep a professional stance on your approach to the entire situation. Answer each reproach with a pre-planned solution on how you plan to overcome a certain obstacle. Your proposed solution should be as detailed as possible and applicable specifically to you. Lastly, remember to never leave room for people, especially your investors, to doubt your capabilities.

3

Trust in Your Business Plan

Often, you will be faced with an unexpected resolution. You are denied the possible investment, and you will lose this opportunity. At this point, discouragement is inevitable, but don't let it linger.

Getting turned down is part of the path to success. So – get off your ass and start finding other investors.

Try out other opportunities. Don't trap yourself with the thought that losing one investment means that you won't get a future investment. In reality, your next deal might be an even better deal than before. A tone of desperation, never-ceasing calls to your investors' office, and continuous approaches to gaining the trust of your investor is never a good sign.

As an alternative, stick to your business plan, stand by your own word, and take every chance to bring more credibility towards yourself and your business.

4

Persuasion and Your Business Proposal

Throughout your speech, aim to draw a picture for your investors. Allow them to envision your idea and your perspective on how this business will be run and how this business will succeed in the market.

Here are some of the points that you have to discuss within your concrete business proposal:

A) Overview of the Startup: discuss how your business operates, your product/service, the amount of competition in the same niche market, and your mission statement and vision;

B) Short-Term and Long-Term Goals for your startup: clearly state your goals for your company and address a list of methods which you will use to tackle specific goals in the future,

C) Have A Unique Selling Proposition (USP): every company has its own specialty and target audience,

D) "How You Will Get The Customers": identify multiple marketing strategies for how you will reach out to potential customers and how you will generate a loyal community to your startup/brand/business,

E) Product/Service: if you are selling a product, make sure to create an organized sheet with every item (for example, your suppliers would need to know what materials you are asking for) listed in detail; if you are providing a service, your business plan should encompass all reasons why your particular service has a high demand in the market and why it is worth investing in.

F) Compare/Contrast Yourself to Adult Prospects: drill in the fact that you are young and full of ideas; shut down any investor's assumption that you are inexperienced or uneducated with proof that you can handle yourself just as well as any other adult. It's unfair that you have to compete with adults and their resources, but your youth can end up as an advantage rather than a disadvantage if you sell it well.

Lastly, consider one additional piece of advice. When you deliver your business proposal, never utter the phrase "I need xxx dollars" in your speech. This is the line that will kill your business proposal immediately. This proposal may make investors look at you as a child asking for money.

Instead of asking for money, end your speech by asking for advice. Have the mindset of "I want to learn", "I want to improve" and "Maybe I can learn something for this experienced person" instead of "let me lick their boots until I get the money I need because there is nothing I can learn from them." Be open-minded to EVERY POTENTIAL INVESTOR. With asking for advice, you've set your investors on a pedestal. Asking for advice indirectly suggests that you respect the experience of your investors in this situation – AND you are willing to learn and make changes to your pitch or your business model based on their advice.

5. Formulating a Team

Vogue editor-in-chief and style mogul Anna Wintour has repeatedly stated that "you are nothing without your team." And that is damn true.

During the first few months of your startup, you might be able to juggle customizing your website, packaging orders, marketing on multiple social media platforms, and running your business in a full circle. To run a business is not an easy feat and balancing a stressful workload all by yourself might not be the best way to manage a business.

Tips?

Understand that you don't have to do it all by yourself. Hire a copywriter online on freelancer.com or indeed.com to write content for your blog or a graphic designer to create your Facebook advertisement. Find a friend or family member who are willing to give professional advice on how to improve your startup, or hire them to help you with a section of the company.

How To Hire Your Friend or Family Member?

Starting a business with the help of a friend or family member can be both a positive and a negative thing.

Hiring, working, and doing business with friends and family can become a disorganized and chaotic mess. Often times with business situations including friends or family businesses, people clash due to the fact that there is a lack of company hierarchy.

If the people that are working together are closely related or acquainted, they will be brutally honest. In one scenario, the honesty can damage a level of respect that is expected in a traditional workplace despite the close relations. In another scenario, the honesty can be advantageous; speaking your opinions can result in higher productivity and stronger steps towards the end goal.

Regardless of the difficulties, negotiation and unbiased decision-making is the key. Be straight-forward with your responses and opinions, but definitely be mindful of your tone of voice if you think that you might be coming off as unnecessarily harsh and unappreciative.

Essentially, you have to determine the line between a professional relationship and a family relationship, especially the time to get to work and get serious.

The Contract Twist

During the first three months of my photography business. I earned approximately 1K in profit taking photos for clients, who were mostly close friends or acquaintances. However, because I faced a reoccurring issue of clients trying to negotiate package prices and having other pricing concerns, I hired a friend to help me write a contract for future clients.

The contract ensures that clients will follow the guidelines of each photography package, follow through on payments and ensures that my photographs would not be utilized for any ill purposes.

The so-called 'contract' was not legal to say the least, but it was a binding form that ensured that my clients held up their agreements. To conclude, if you have to write and sign a document to avoid confusion or future misinformation with clients or employees, do it!

Your Team Is Everything

Building your team requires careful selection of each member, what they bring to the table, and an assessment of how their diverse personalities will shape the company. You want people that you can listen to and people that aren't afraid to step up and speak up.

One of the things that I've realized is that leadership isn't just the big hurrah of holding the torch and running the herd. The ability to be observant and to analyze every individual's specialty can become useful. When you identify someone's talent or skill, prompt them to incorporate it in discussions, meetings, or any aspect of your business. Involving everyone and using every employee to the best of his/her ability is one in many skills that differentiate a follower from a leader.

6. You Launched Your Business. What Now?

Keep it afloat.

Everyone can launch a business, but only a few have the ability to keep their company hovering above turbulent waters and in the competitive range of the market.

How do you survive and grow?

1

Learn

There is a reason why successful entrepreneurs pair their breakfast and coffee with a newspaper. In order to familiarize yourself with the ever-growing industry and the interconnected communities that we live in, learn more so that you can incorporate new knowledge into the growth of your business.

Being a teenager means that you have time – time to make mistakes, try new things, and gain experience. You might end up doing a lot of stuff for free in the beginning to help you gain experience, but eventually you can charge your clients more when you become a so-called 'expert' in your field.

2

Adapt To Trends

With a mindful foot in the foundation of your business (revisit your mission statement and vision from time to time), don't be afraid to adapt to cultural and societal trends. The booming industry of social media has taken over the world in a flash, and companies have transferred to online platforms and websites to better connect with their consumers and communicate with their audiences.

It's important for businesses to adapt to trends, because whatever is trending is CAPTURING PEOPLE'S ATTENTION.

Your goal as a business is the same: you want to adapt your product/service to those trends. Why? Because everyone wants to hop on the trend wagon. They want to go to the same places that their favorite celebrity has traveled to, purchase the same hydro flask that all the VSCO girls have, and show off their AirForce Ones so that they can be included in this 'community' of sorts.

Think about it. Why are retailers like Revolve spending their money to have their clothes promoted by Instagram influencers, trending YouTubers, and TikTok stars? It's because they have a similar target audience, and a company can better target these potential customers through a well-connected and popular influencer or celebrity.

3

Invest In Yourself

The best that you can invest in is – essentially – yourself. This means that you are the person that is believing in you when no one else does.

Many entrepreneurs start by making money themselves, and they don't have an entire team or employees like a businessperson. They're alone, which means that they have to depend on themselves.

Teenage entrepreneurs will also be in the same situation where they have to believe in themselves and their business. Not giving up on your goals, whether it is becoming a singer or starting a clothing brand, is the number one strategy that will help you persevere and make it through your entrepreneurship journey towards success.

Most teenagers (and adults, too) won't push through those tough times, but making it through those difficult moments can be rewarding in the future of your business.

2
Let's Work (Il)legally!

I am a teenager and I want to start working, but how can I do so legally?

Ambitious, driven, and ready to earn some extra money?

Well, all I ask is that you leave all your expectations at the door. Come in, grab a chair, and make yourself at home – we've got a few problems to discuss.

Hopefully (yes, hopefully), teenagers are well aware that the legal working age in most international countries is 18. A few of the benefits reaped from working at a young age would include building your skill sets in a particular niche or in different industries, connecting with professionals or employers, tallying early working experience, and putting a foot forward to acquaint yourself with working life. Besides, balancing a part-time job and schoolwork can train young adults to be more organized, learn how to handle problems at work, interact with people with different personalities and backgrounds, and be further prepared for the challenge of impending adulthood.

Category One: **Online**

Freelance, selling your own online courses, online consulting, photography services, write for a blog or newspaper company, copywriting, designing posters, booking gigs, social media manager, social media consultant, social media influencer, start a podcast, etc.

Category Two: **Real-World Job**

Internships, part-time jobs, full-time jobs, babysitting, tutoring, cleaning a hotel room, retail sales, making sandwiches at Subway, a lifeguard at a country club, a receptionist at a restaurant, etc.

Before I turned 16, I did a bunch of unconventional jobs outlined in Category One. I started my photography business, worked with a Chinese manufacturing company to shoot marketing ads during the COVID-19 outbreak, and shot videos for private parties at local restaurants and bars. As someone living in China, the Category Two: Hired For a REAL-WORLD Job is not nearly in reach before the age of 16 or 18 compared to the US, which legally allowed age 14+ minors to work legally for a certain amount of hours only.

I know, I know… you think that all my Category One work has already given me enough real-world experience given the current uprising of tech giants and a future of innovation, but hear me out. The thing about Category Two is that they let you have a chance to be in an environment where you can interact with other people. Category Two encompasses every aspect of working life and is a great place to start for many teenagers who want to experience what "having a job" is like.

You might think that you never want to work at a fast-food chain like Chipotle or McDonald's, and that's okay.

9/10 times you will be rejected from higher-paying and full-time jobs due to your lack of experience and basic student profile. Almost every single industry requires some level of experience, and who doesn't want to hire the best out of the best? (unless you can't afford them)

This is why it is important to make a realistic and knowledgeable decision about your first few jobs as you get ready to climb the corporate ladder up to your dream job.

Profile One – Cora Jean

Target Goal: Marketing CEO at Elle Magazine

Age: 16

Homework: listened to podcasts featuring former Elle Magazine editor-in-chiefs or department heads, downloaded the online pdf on Magazine Publishing for Dummies to familiarize with the fashion publishing industry, read up on Elle Magazine, Women's Wear Daily, and other fashion resources, tried to get in contact with previous interns working at Elle Magazine, and sent emails to the internship coordinator, HR department (be persistent and email until you get a reply!), or the editor-in-chief (grab your guts and give it a go).

Previous Experience: interning in fashion closet, editorial, and retail locally

Job Applying To: Fashion Intern at Elle Magazine

How To Apply For A Job – "The Underaged Edition"
Lesson One: NEVER Climb The Corporate Ladder BLIND

Imagine if you were the internship coordinator and Elle Magazine was looking for "highly qualified and experienced individuals in the fashion industry": would you choose someone with a CV that points out that they worked in McDonalds for three weeks? It's an obvious no.

Starting off from the wrong foot can cause you to lose precious time to devote to something more important. Wasting your time in a fast food chain will not boost your CV or resume up a notch in 'experience level'.

While some individuals have landed internships without any work experience, it's always better to have some level of work experience to leverage your capabilities.

In order to climb the corporate ladder effectively, you have to look ahead and see your goals from a mile away. Without a clear understanding of what position you want to achieve in a specific industry or what status you want to earn in general society, DO NOT go blindly applying to fifty companies that you have never heard about. Be sure that you have a clear mind map for your future in order to move forward with applying for jobs or internships.

Target and apply for jobs that are related to your passion or the industry you want to work in. For the sake of explanation, I created a profile above (which can possibly be turned into a CV later) with 16-year-old Cora Jean. She has done local work with fashion closet, editorial, and retail, which can definitely be a strength if she wants to earn an internship at Elle Magazine. The previous work experience she listed are all within the fashion industry, which helps recruiters understand that Jean is especially passionate and hard-working towards a fashion career.

Another situation can be that you simply want to get a job to jumpstart your work experience. Even if you are working at a salad bar or the cashier in a job with no relation to your future ambitions, it still counts as experience. Future employers may be surprised to learn that you started to work at such a young age, because it indicates that you are ambitious and hard working.

Lesson Two: *Do Your Homework BEFORE You Apply For A Job*

You never want to apply for a company if you know nothing about them. So, do some research about how their company is run, who is on the executive team or head of departments, what the CEO of the company is like, and the personal experiences of previous or current interns at that company.

In her profile, Jean listed everything that she did to prepare for her Elle Magazine internship, from contacting previous interns to getting to know more about fashion publishing as a whole. Doing the research and the learning process can be the ultimate up-factor that demonstrates your professional and dedicated approach to the industry.

After hopefully landing an interview, show up at the interview with a physical copy of your resume and prepare to be asked all different kinds of questions.

With a basic set of knowledge about the company and the industry before arriving at the interview, you have an advantage over other job candidates that didn't do full-length research and studying. The interviewers tend to like somebody that knows the in-and-outs of their company, so it's easier for you to fit right in and get to work.

Supermodel Cindy Crawford pointed out the importance of "doing your homework" during the 2019 Vogue's Forces of Fashion conference. "If I know that this photographer shoots this way, when I get to set, I kind of already know what language we might be speaking that day. As opposed to walking in and not knowing anything about the editor or the designer or the photographer."

Every job requires some substantial amount of knowledge and understanding of the company, the employees, the employers, the competitors, the overall industry, etc.

Lesson Three: *Jumping Past Age Barriers*

To be honest, there are not a lot of resources and workplaces that allow underaged teenagers to work. Internships or potential Category Two jobs are only available once you are an undergraduate in university or a high school graduate, which means you probably already reached the 18-year-old mark. Yet, teenagers can try their best to get around the system.

Tip 1

Build Your Resume

Although you can't get past child labor laws or jump the fence on the minimum age of employment in your country, my suggestion is to start building your resume and CV in the working 'experience' section. By tackling a few Category One jobs, starting a fundraiser, or beginning your own small business, you can always add those accomplishments onto your resume.

Tip 2

Inquire First If There Is An Age Restriction

CAUTION ADVICE: It's not easy to convince companies to hire minors, because they already have rules that state the age restriction. That doesn't mean that you cannot try inquiring about a job opening.

Contact the recruiter and ask them whether or not they hire minors. In some cases, grocery stores and fast food chains can have an age restriction of 14+. Other bigger companies may also accept your application or even hire you, if you have a parent/guardian's permission.

In my opinion, it's always better to apply for internships as a teenager, because 1) you have a chance to learn, 2) you have a chance to adapt to the workspace and a working environment, and 3) there are more internship opportunities in bigger companies for younger people.

Tip 3

Ask Others That Have Worked Underaged

Imagine that a small social media consulting firm has hired your older brother when he was 14 as a content creator for their social media pages. It's likely that the same social media consulting firm will hire other 14-year-olds. Asking others that have had similar work experience or are in the same situation you are currently in now can minimize your time searching for companies that might end up rejecting you due to your age.

Tip 4

Get People To Vouch For You

Establishing a strong connection with a former or current employee (or possibly a respected individual in the industry) can also push you one step closer to getting the job. Tie a mutual friend into the conversation of your interview, and your interview might know the person you are referring to.

Having credible individuals in the industry or company vouch for you despite your age will prove that you have the capabilities to do well in that job, and you have already earned the respect and approval of another person (that the recruiter may also know).

Tip 5

Your Age Is Your Argument

Here's a bit of story time. Two years ago, an online friend recommended me to become a part of the new ambassadors' team at NuSkin Enterprise. After jumping on three business calls with a recruiter from NuSkin, I revealed my age – 14.

As soon as I revealed my age, the other end of the phone began to have obvious doubts. Being young has its disadvantages if you are looking for a freelancing job, internship, or even becoming a part of an ambassador's program. What you should do is try your best to lessen those doubts with reassurance:

I understand that you have doubts about my age. However, I believe that my age can be extremely beneficial for your company, because your company targets a younger audience. The best way to understand what young people need is to have an actual adolescent in the team. If you go straight to the source, you don't have to spend money on advertisements and asking teenagers to do surveys."

Use your age as the central argument of WHY it further improves your application and WHY you should be the one that gets the job. In reality, your age can be your disadvantage, but nonetheless, you can still make your argument for why you are a perfect candidate for the job. Your argument can be a 'suggestion' that will sway your recruiter's final decision from left to right.

Towards the end of the conversation, the recruiter might say something like "yes, I will check with my supervisor... I will call you back" or "no, thank you, our company only accepts applicants above 18 (or another age depending on the country or company policies)."

The most important thing is to make your argument but accept rejection (which I did – the NuSkin recruiter assured that I could reapply to be an ambassador when I turned 16). Some companies are simply not open to allowing underaged individuals be a part of their company, but as soon as you find employers or recruiters that are willing to give you a chance – give 110% to the job to ensure your employer or recruiter that they made the right decision to hire you.

Here is an example of an email response that I got for my NuSkin ambassador program application:

From: ▮▮▮▮▮▮▮▮
Sent: Thursday, July 4, 2019 1:45:38 PM
To: Shirley Wang

Subject: RE: NUSKIN brand information

Shirley

Thank you for your time this morning on the phone. Unfortunately, until you are at least 16 yr 9 months we cannot officially register you as a brand ambassador on the platform. However, I just wanted to say you will be awesome and please stay connected with Katie and request access to the closed Facebook group (in normal circumstances you need to a brand ambassador to get access to the group) but we will accept you in.

So yes, please stay connect you will see what the girls are doing and when you are old enough, we will certainly welcome you with open arms.

Tip 6

Go For It

You can't complain that "they'll never accept me because I'm underaged." Well. You've never tried applying. So, start getting in contact with the manager of the place you want to work at (restaurant, company, firm, etc.) and ask for a job.

It never hurts to ask.

Lesson Four: Toughen Up For Likely Rejections and Try Again

Receiving a rejection letter or no reply does not mean that you are destined to be a failure in this industry. What it means is that 1) you did not try hard enough to pursue that job, 2) you did not want it badly enough, or 3) that company was not the right fit for you or vice versa.

Many individuals give up after one rejection letter, burying their face in a pint of ice cream or hitting the extreme button and sending negative emails back to the company recruiter on impulse due to the blow of rejection. This will only make you feel worse and indicate that you are not mature enough.

Worse-case scenarios can include another rejection if you ever decide to apply for a job at the same company again when you are of age, especially if the same recruiter remembers your 'hate-mail' years later. Whilst a negative email or letter won't significantly hurt you to the point of getting blacklisted in an entire industry, you can still be creating a bad reputation for yourself that will stick.

So, don't do it.

Below is a step-by-step guide on what you should be doing.

How To Combat Rejection

STEP ONE: In a situation of rejection, hold yourself together and write a sincere thank-you-for-your-consideration-and-time letter/email back to the company recruiter.

STEP TWO: Try again. I would suggest that you send out ten applications at once, because probably only two out of the ten will give you a reply. Since many applicants use email and a recruiter (or whoever you are sending the email to) gets hundreds of emails per day, they might delete your email in less than three seconds. Instead, mail a neatly hand-written or a typed letter to the company. The response to physical format application is better, because most young adults and teenagers would not choose the mailing process when they can send an email in a matter of a button.

STEP THREE: Wait for a reply. This make take around two to four weeks max. If there is no reply, assume that the person did not like your application, and leave it at that.

NOTE: A letter of rejection or no letter back at all is a learning process. How you react to rejection will determine who you become in the future. Let your head lead instead of your emotions in this circumstance and keep applying till you get the job or internship you want.

The most important quality of entrepreneurship is persistence and perseverance, especially in teenage entrepreneurs. Teenagers can often have impulsive or risk-taking behavior, which means that there is a higher likelihood for failure.

The act of overcoming obstacles, accepting your mistakes and learning from them, and facing constant rejection before trying again – that is what a successful entrepreneur would do. They would not give up no matter the amount of backlash or the number of rejections. The faster that a teenage entrepreneur can accept rejection, the faster they can get up again and make their business better.

How To Freelance (and why teens can do it too)

At least in the United States, a minor or underaged teenager cannot be bound by a contract. If necessary, it is best to have your parents enter a contract for you (under their name) to begin working for a company or a person.

Some freelancing websites, such as freelancer.com or upwork.com, are not all contract-based jobs, but they need you to sign up with a PayPal account or credit card.

Other freelancing websites, including problogger.com, allows freelancers to choose between contracts, part-time, or freelance options when scrolling through jobs. Teenagers can easily filter through the job list and choose the freelance or part-time option instead of the contract option.

Freelancing can easily become a part-time job and a great opportunity for teenagers to start using their skills to earn money. There are many different types of freelance work, including graphic design, copywriting, proofreading, etc.

In a freelancing website, you apply for a job posted by an employer, you do the job, you hand in your work, and you get the money via credit card or PayPal.

It is much quicker than you would expect, and there is not a lot of interaction between employer and freelancer, which can help you avoid the entire 'underage' conversation. As long as the work you hand in passes your employer's expectations, then you get the money.

Have A Bottom Line and Negotiate

You're young, so how do you make sure that a colleague or the boss of your freelancing or internship job is not treating you unfairly or poorly due to your 'inexperience' and age?

Underaged teenagers do not have the same qualifications and experience level as a 25-year-old, which means that they have to put in more effort to prove themselves and get the position they want.

Negotiate the best deal for yourself with your employer. Argue for what you want in a nice and suggestive tone. For instance, it could that you want to do the paid internship like the older interns, and you are trying to get your employer's permission.

Another point that I want to stress is that you need to have a bottom line for every job. This is especially important for teenagers that are beginning in an industry and want to thrive; they have to begin by setting down some ground rules for themselves and what they want to achieve.

Depending on an individual, their bottom line can range from constant signs of disrespect to even harassment. You have to be firm about your bottom line and make a serious decision of whether or not you want to back out of a job if it passes your bottom line.

Working a job is a whole new world for any teenager – and a majority of you have to start from scratch. Start by doing the dirty dishes in the back of the kitchen or untangling clothing lines in a closet. Any job, from freelance to internships, is a form of experience. Building up that experience is what you are shooting for, but teenagers still have to be aware and careful about what kind of workplace environment they are getting involved in.

3
Teenage Entrepreneur Stories

*I have seen other teenagers launch their own successful businesses...
but how did they do it?*

In this chapter, we're diving right behind the red theater curtains to the real show: the behind-the-scenes of successful teenagers and young adults running their own businesses.

1
Paola Ochoa:
Social Media Marketer of Socials by Paola

Paola is currently a student at the Fashion Institute of Design and Merchandising and the founder of Socials By Paola and Teen Boss Babes, which she launched at the age of 16.

Socials by Paola (SBP) is a social media agency in order to help other content creators to who want to learn new skills or get social media help, including Instagram management to YouTube content creation. After launching SBP, she created Teen Boss Babes (TBB), which is a community for young teen entrepreneurs who want to start their own business or build their own personal brand. Both businesses are positive communities for young and aspiring female entrepreneurs.

1. What was the process of launching and running your brand/business?

I quickly just made Instagram and started from there to launch SBP. I also went straight into joining Facebook groups and shared my business services. As I'm running SBP, I make sure I make it like feel like it is a part of my daily life and not just work. Now for TBB, I took more time to create my launch day and how I wanted it to be. I started TBB three months before even mentioning it, so it was much more time and dedication at the beginning.

2. What are some of the struggles that you encountered while you were trying to launch your business?

For SBP, the first main struggle was being able to reach out and marketing myself to other women. I had to take a lot of time from my day to look through Facebook groups and share my services. For TBB, I did not reach any struggles because I was able to learn from my past mistakes.

3. How do you balance your businesses with schoolwork?

When I am in school, I always make sure to still put my business as a priority. When I finish any schoolwork, I make sure to move onto answering DMs, working on client work, or posting content.

4. What is your opinion on teenagers starting businesses and what is your advice to teens that also want to get into the job market before 18?

I feel like it is very important for teens to start their business. If that is something they want to start doing, they can do it, and no one should stop them. That is exactly the reason why I am creating TBB, because I want young entrepreneurs to feel safe and heard to start their own businesses.

Hedy Zhou:

Happily, Hedy Blogger & Graphic Designer

Hedy started running a lifestyle blog/brand called Happily, Hedy and a graphic design studio at the age of 16. Her brand mission is to empower young women to go after their dreams and live their best life, so her blog content is focused on areas of self-care and self-development, as well as general lifestyle categories (style, food, books, etc.).

1. How did you start Happily, Hedy the blog?

    I initially started several blogs before I decided to stick to one. There were like three others which I discontinued, but I did learn a lot from each one. After setting up so many previous blogs, it helped me set up new blogs and they helped build up my experience, so I was able to make Happily, Hedy successful.

2. What went on behind-the-scenes of Happily, Hedy the blog?

    I guess the biggest thing I did was research. Since there are so many resources online, I literally put together a folder with all the freebies I could find. I still have the folder and it's PACKED with stuff (things I haven't even gotten the chance to go through too). I reached a point where the new things I looked up just repeated stuff I previously read about already, so I kind of knew I found everything I possibly could in that area.

    As I researched, I also got my website/blog set up. I love building websites (I'm a graphic designer, after all) and I do want to emphasize how important they are. A website is where your potential customer is going to find all your work, contact info, and social media. It really builds you that professional presence online.

After all, the first thing people do to learn more about your business is Google it. You don't necessarily need to pay for a domain/hosting until you are sure you're serious about your business – I started on a free platform for a while and was still able to grow it successfully. Of course, there's a point where if you want to really make it big, you're going to have to invest more than just your time.

3. What are your thoughts on teenagers/young adults dabbling in entrepreneurship?

I love it and think more teens should be exploring entrepreneurship! It's definitely a rewarding experience as you really do learn a lot from it. You can literally take any passion of yours and turn it into a business: just be creative, and don't give up. Consistency is key and celebrate every little win because they do build up.

3
Beatrice Naujalyte:
The Bliss Bean Blogger & Photography Business Owner

Beatrice Naujalyte started her own photography business in Madison, Wisconsin at the age of 16. Her photographs are mostly senior portraits, but she also does couples shoots, family shoots, headshots, etc. She also runs a blog, The Bliss Bean, based on her passion for productive routines and helping others nurture a healthy mindset.

1. What inspired/prompted you to launch your photography business?

I've always been drawn to creating, in whatever form that manifested itself throughout my life. My parents tell me that when I was little I'd walk around with a digital camera and snap seemingly random photos of furniture around the house. Later, when they'd look through the camera roll, they'd be surprised at the creativity and effort I put into composing those shots.

As I grew up, I continued taking photos as a hobby. I was the designated family vacation photographer and videographer. I jumped at any opportunity in school to create photo or video projects. And, starting in middle school, I dabbled in blogging and took photos to accompany my posts.

Starting a photography business was not really on my radar, and I have to say it happened quite by accident. The summer before my junior year (I was 16), a friend asked if I did senior portraits, and I honestly answered that I'd never taken senior photos, but I'd be totally down to try. Luckily for her (because I had zero experience at that point!), she ended up choosing another photographer, but she kindly offered to let me practice on her.

It was completely new territory for me. I had no idea how to pose someone for photos, I had my aperture at the wrong setting throughout the entire shoot, and my editing wasn't great, to put it gently. But my very first portrait shoot sparked something in me, and I knew I needed to follow that spark. I started an Instagram account, put out a call for models to practice on, and did a few practice shoots before I decided that I was ready to start charging a fee. Basically, I put together a graphic with some of the practice photos I'd taken, wrote out my offering, and put it out there on Instagram and Facebook.

That first season, I mainly only shot for friends or acquaintances I knew from middle school. The next year, however, things quickly started growing and through word-of-mouth and a growing portfolio, I started getting more and more clients.

2. What is your photography business about, what is your goal or purpose from starting this business, and how would you describe your business to people who have never heard of it?

This business is quite straightforward, and I guess my goal at the start was to find a way to utilize my passion for photography in a way that earned me money. It was my part-time job throughout high school, and it was not only more lucrative but 100x more enjoyable than I think working a traditional part-time job would have been.

I thrive in an environment where I can work by myself and manage my own time and responsibilities, so the process of running a business, while at times stressful, made me deeply happy.

Another goal of mine was to improve my photography skills and looking back at my early work (just two years ago), compared to now, there is a world of difference. Some of that has come as a result of watching photography tutorials or reading up on the technical aspects of the craft, but the majority of it is due to the sheer amount of practice that this business has given me.

I've done more than 40 senior portrait shoots to date, and every aspect of my service, from how I shoot and edit to how I communicate with clients, has improved as a result.

3. How do you price your photographs?

When I first started, I had a very simple pricing system. I had one offering at one price, which I gradually raised as my skills improved and demand grew.

For the second year, I expanded my offerings and created a three-tier system with packages that offer different amounts of photos, shooting time, locations, and outfits. This proved to be a really successful strategy because all three packages were about equally popular. I was able to attract clients with different budgets.

As for getting clients, as I mentioned before, I started with taking photos for my friends, then acquaintances, then schoolmates, and I am now at a point where I am taking photos for students from other schools or even other cities, who heard about me from a previous client or who found my work on Instagram.

4. What's your experience with blogging and tell me more about your blog, The Bliss Bean?

I've experimented with blogging since Grade 7. Since then, my multiple blogs have varied in their focus (my first blog was about arts and crafts projects), but they've all given me an outlet to do what I truly love – create.

I wrote my very first post for my current blog, The Bliss Bean, in July 2017. Originally, I intended for it to be a health and wellness blog. At the time, I was fascinated with nutrition and exercise, in a way that seemed innocent enough, but at the heart of it, was unhealthy. It's interesting to look back on my archive of posts, because my blog is a window into how I grew up, overcame some mental health struggles, and found that my true passion came from helping people be more productive and mindful, and thus live happier lives.

5. What are some of your struggles that you encountered while you were trying to launch your photography business or YouTube channel?

With my photography business, it was a challenge to dive headfirst into something I had very little experience with. Sure, I knew more or less how to take photos, but I wasn't sure how to design a service, market myself, and create a client experience.

As an introvert, interacting with clients during photoshoots was really intimidating to me. I still get nervous before shoots! But I can confidently say I've gotten better at it and feel much more comfortable during shoots, which in turn makes my clients feel more comfortable and relaxed, resulting in better photos!

With my YouTube channel, it was certainly a struggle to persevere even when I had next to zero results. I uploaded my first video in April 2018, which was seven months and 25 videos later, and I finally reached 100 subscribers. Looking back, I'm honestly amazed that I stuck with it for so long, but I guess your measurement of success grows as your success increases. I'm so proud of my past self for pushing through it and continuing to put out content even when I wasn't getting much of a response. At this point, I can say that it definitely paid off.

6. How do you keep on track with creating new content and being productive?

I firmly believe in the power of systems and self-discipline. Simply put, I don't have to motivate myself much to keep creating new content and being productive, because I've created systems and routines that automate that for me.

I don't negotiate with myself over whether I should do something for my business, because it's the next thing on my to-do list, and thus, I simply have to do it. I could talk for hours and hours about all of the little habits and tools that I use to stay organized and productive, but that's what my YouTube channel is for!

To summarize it, I am a very careful planner. In terms of my life, I plan out my week every Sunday, and start each day with a clear to-do list to tackle. For my photography business, I use a Trello board to organize clients, whose shoots are all at different stages of completion, and for my YouTube channel, I use a content calendar to schedule videos, newsletters, and social media posts, and track the progress of each piece of content. I also utilize a technique called time tracking to keep me accountable and aware of where my time is going. That and paired with the Pomodoro technique (working in 25-minute intervals of time with breaks in between), helps me work more efficiently without getting tired.

7. How well do you think high school has prepared teenagers for pursuing real-world jobs?

    I think that in high school we are too often presented with the same life script to follow. There was plenty of guidance in applying to colleges, looking for internships, and making yourself career-ready, but there was rarely any encouragement to explore alternative options or to create your own job. When I took a personal finance class, I was disappointed that there was no mention of self-employment. How do I start a business? File taxes as a freelancer?

8. What are your suggestions to other teenagers that want to start their own YouTube channel?

    I've often felt discouraged or embarrassed by my desire to pursue YouTube. I felt like it was such a cliché dream, or that people would see me as desperate for attention.

Any time I feel like this, I just have to remind myself of why I do what I do. I have a bunch of messages and comments of gratitude printed out and taped to the wall in my bedroom. I am slowly becoming more and more confident in my purpose, and I know that the work I do is meaningful and genuinely improves others' lives. I would encourage any teenagers who are looking to start a business of some sort to get clear on their purpose first. That'll be the best motivation to keep you going (even when it takes 7 months to reach 100 subscribers!).

4
Ellie Everett: CEO of Nudie Beauty

It's been seven years since Ellie started her own skin care brand, Nudie Beauty, at the age of 12. The South Australian business owner is now 19-year-old, and lives in Adelaide.

1. Tell us the story that sparked the idea of your brand, especially at age 12.

    I started my business in Waikerie, South Australia at the age of 12, which was back in 2013. I created a whipped body butter for my mum as a present for Mother's Day, and she soon mentioned that I should sell them. It took me a month or so before I began to seriously consider it, and I then started researching product recipes and tutorials (primarily through YouTube) to develop my understanding of the products and the ingredients that would need to be purchased.

2. Explain the process of starting your business venture.

    My mum was the one who really believed in me and propelled the whole journey. She gave me a couple of hundred dollars (~$300) in the beginning to get me started up. For the first few years, she would take me to every market and would sit with me all day!

With the money she gave me, I bought an outdoor umbrella for coverage at markets, a trestle table, tablecloth, beeswax, shea butter, olive oil, some essential oil, and then jars for the products. It doesn't sound like much, but it goes to show that you really don't need much to start a business if you are willing to go through the growth process, which can be slow at first.

In late 2015, after about three years of selling at craft markets, I decided to also open up an online store through Etsy. I soon switched to my own domain as I wanted to create my own website and make my online presence exactly how I wanted. This was around the same time that I began to experiment with selling bath products, such as bath bombs, and also soap, which are now favored over the original skincare.

3. Why focus on skin care for your brand?

Off the bat, my product line consisted of just face creams, lip balm, body butter, and also some scrubs.

The reason I settled on crafting skincare was because at the time, back in 2013, there were not nearly as many independent creators of these kinds of products, so I wanted to fill the gaps that was very much present, especially around my local area. Also, I realized that a lot of the products that were commercially available were often formulated with nasty chemicals, unnecessary additives, and synthetic fragrances.

4. How do you generate income with your business?

I make an effort to still attend markets regularly as I consider it an effective way of increasing my local brand awareness, which can then translate into more site traffic.

When first opening my Etsy store, it took about three or four months before getting my first order and it was of just one product, but I was so excited. Online sales then began to slowly build, and they always peak in certain times of the year, but I do find that sales volume still fluctuates greatly between months which I do struggle to maintain.

I still get the same thrill, especially in the beginning from every single order that comes through, and I deeply appreciate my customers' support of my business.

Another selling point for me is through wholesale orders to stocks. There have been many occasions where I have gained a new stock relationship by actually reaching out to a business that I'd had my eye on, and simply telling my story and asking if they'd be interested in seeing some samples. More often than not, business will be willing to support you – especially if they are local – and the worst that can really happen is they say no, and if that does happen, just move on!

5. You started your business at age 12, so what is your advice on starting businesses at such a young age?

One of my motivators to start at such a young age is because I otherwise had no other way to make money at my age, unless I hand cut apricots in the holidays with the other kids. My advice would be to take a critical look at what problems you encounter during day to day life and try to develop a product or service to overcome these issues.

Typically, if there is a problem that you experience, chances are other people are too, and if you are able to spot that opportunity, you will be able to deliver a product/service for a problem that your potential consumers didn't even know they had! Through innovation into your business practices, you will be able to target a niche market, and chances are, you'll grow the business quicker.

5
Tricia Panlaqui (Justricia):
YouTuber & Social Media Influencer

Tricia is a YouTube star and a content creator of lifestyle vlogs, beauty videos, and fashion tutorials. Through her YouTube channel, justricia, she has created a career path for herself. One of her videos, "My First Youtube Paycheck + How To Make Money On Youtube 2018" received three million views in early 2018.

1. Tell us about how your YouTube channel has grown over the years.

    My social media journey began when I was 11 years old. I had just discovered what social media was and quickly found interest in what they did. It inspired me to create an Instagram account in the summer of 2014 and use my iPhone to film short 15 second videos about my outfits and beauty products. I spent my summer creating these videos and learned to eventually be comfortable around the camera. By the end of the summer, I had acquired a couple thousand followers, and decided to continue this hobby during the school year.

    By summer of 2015, I had been used to making videos for a year and created my YouTube channel. I posted my first video "15 Second Walmart Shopping Spree!" on May 18, 2015.

    I inconsistently uploaded every few months, and posted my last Instagram video at the end of 2016, as I started high school. My "What I Got For Christmas & 15th Birthday Haul 2017!" had acquired 20,000 views overnight, which was nothing like I had seen before. This video made me realize that there is an audience of people out there who are genuinely interested in what I was posting, and it made me consider picking up the hobby again.

I began 2018 with 15,000 subscribers. I set my goal to post every week of 2018 and ended the year with over 200,000. I was mind blown, overwhelmed, happy, and scared with the amount of growth, change, and feedback I received in this one year.

In 2018, I realized I could make money off of this hobby, so I got my first sponsorships, filed my first taxes, my first video to reach a million views, and many more milestones. In the summer of 2018, I moved to the Philippines. This drastic change affected my sponsorships, monetization, and how often I was able to upload. After getting adjusted to my new life, I continued posting weekly in 2019 and received my hard-earned YouTube plaque, and worked with brands I didn't think would ever notice me.

Now in 2020, I have been exposed to even bigger opportunities, featured in the newspaper and commercials, and am continuing to upload videos weekly with the same passion and drive I felt as that young 11-year-old girl in my room.

As I graduate high school this year, I feel reassured and happy knowing that the community I have created has watched me, stayed with me, and supported me through all my years of high school.

The process has allowed me to grow in confidence and in knowledge, taught me to be creative, positive, and headstrong. I cannot imagine my life without my YouTube. I value it and am more than thankful for everything it has taught me.

2. What prompted you to monetize and start earning money from your own YouTube channel at such a young age?

My YouTube channel started as a hobby that I dedicated much of my free time into as a child. I didn't realize that my favorite hobby could turn into a source of income. I was extremely happy and satisfied just being able to make and post videos. I gained inspiration from watching other YouTubers, and eventually built up courage to start my own. I started off on Instagram at the age of 11, and had over 50,000 followers by 12, before switching over to YouTube.

3. What is your YouTube channel's goal or message to your audience?

The goal of my YouTube channel is not only to entertain people, but hopefully make them happy and allow them to feel inspired. I have a few videos on my channel dedicated to helping people start and grow a YouTube channel, which are now my most viewed videos on my channel. These are my favorite videos to create, because the comments make me realize that my content can help and inspire others to do what they love. I have always hoped to spread positivity.

4. What would you say to other teenagers that want to succeed on YouTube?

To any teens interested in entering the social media industry at a young age, I would only hope for you to enter this field filled with passion and interest, being positive that this is what you want to do. I would hope you do it because you love and enjoy it, not thinking about the business and money side to it.

If you start social media with goals to make an income, your channel will simply not succeed. You must be driven by nothing else but passion, and hold onto it, and always keep it with you. Learn to be confident in yourself. Do not change who you are, it really isn't worth it.

Don't be scared to adventure, explore, or evolve your content, there are no guidelines you need to follow.

Social media is not kind, and cyber bullying is a clear issue, be sure to know your worth and not listen to hateful comments, because the more you grow, the more hate you will receive. Open your ears to constructive criticism, they just want to help you be better. Don't tire yourself out, if you need a break, you are not letting anyone down.

6
Jade Darmawangsa:
Gen Z Entrepreneur & Creative Strategist

At 18, Jade is the CEO and founder of three companies: Personal Brand Journey, EatLike, and The Green Room. As a high school dropout and a millennial entrepreneur, she has amassed an audience of over 300,000 fans on her YouTube channel.

She teaches personal branding, marketing strategies, and provides social media advice through one-on-one coaching calls. Jade's podcast The Raisn Brand was part of iTunes' "Top 100 Business Podcast" in 2018 and she was also named "Creator on the Rise" in YouTube Trending Worldwide.

1. What was your response to the first you received millions of views on one of your videos?

    I remembered the coolest part was meeting people. I suddenly had a ton of friends that were interested in Instagram – like me. I think the access to have as many friends as I wanted to was the most important thing. The viewers were so cool, but the conversations I were having with people were even cooler.

2. Tell us about your creative process for making a YouTube video.

I am a huge believer in not reinventing the wheel. All creating is recreating. What I mean by that is that I don't try to be original – I'm not going to be Hans Zimmer or Picasso!

What I'm really good at is combining two things that have nothing to do with each other into something.

For my video creating process, what I do is I start with 'what do I want to mix?' 'what do I want to create that's already existing in the world, but combining them together can become something even more powerful?'

So, lately what I've been doing is that I find a marketing trend that is cool, such as how TikTokers grow. And then I combine it with something that I love, which is surfing. Then I come up with a vlog or storyline.

So, I really start with 'what do I want people to hear' and 'what am I interested in' and I combine it. I think that's where you get a ton of ideas, because you don't have to become Picasso… you just have to fuse things together. That's what creating really is. It's not about being original. It's about recreating and becoming inspired.

3. What does Darmanation mean to you?

I always say, 'I hope you dominate today.' For me, I left high at a very young age and I never looked back since. Darmanation means dominating life, and just going 110% into your passions.

4. Explain your three businesses.

My holding company is called X8 Media; inside X8, we produce content and products for entrepreneur. We want our products and services to help people create something that is more unconventional.

Whether it's food, TikTok, or YouTube, I just want to as many entrepreneurs become the best at creating something.

At The Green Room (TGR), we produce content for entrepreneurs and creators, and we interview people. At EatLike, our goal is to eat like people that inspire me and other entrepreneurs. At Personal Brand Journey (PBJ), it's one of our product lines where we help entrepreneurs connect with their audience using text message.

5. Can you reflect on your experience of dropping out of high school?

I knew I did not have money for college and my goal was to go to USC in Los Angeles, which is really expensive. If you know that you're probably not going to get in and you can't afford it, why not start now? For my circumstances, college just didn't make sense.

I definitely believe everything happens for a reason. Dropping out of high school was not a hard decision. It sounds very weird – because I should be scared. But in that moment, I never looked back. It was hardly due to the support from YouTube. Instead, it was a combination of not being able to see my future in college and seeing other people strive on the internet. I made my decision with confidence. I don't think I was at all scared. School was just not for me.

6. How do you think your background as a high school dropout came to your advantage or disadvantage when you first started your business in the industry?

For X8 Media, it's a bit of a rocky start to get people to trust you – people were like 'who was this 18-year-old kid?' But you can use your age to your advantage.

A brand that I recently worked for said that I was really young, but the reason they called me up was because they actually wanted me to produce this marketing content and I was the only one that could understand TikTok and YouTube. It's a literal grind to find a positive out of a negative. For my age, I think it became my strength.

There's a new project that I'm shooting for and the reason why they contacted me was because there were people that were more experienced, but they didn't really understand the platform. So, they couldn't make the content to fit the mold. At 18, I might not know lifelong tips and tricks, because I'm not old enough to be a life coach. But I can definitely talk about TikTok and Instagram.

7. Can you describe a time where you had to overcome an obstacle in one of your companies?

One of my companies is called the EatLike. It was just losing a ton of money. I don't like having a business where we go negative every time we grow. It was just really frustrating. It's very normal in a startup world – you're going to lose money, so you have to invest in your products.

For me, the EatLike didn't have enough capital to burn that fast. I had to pause it, currently. It's not a big deal to slow down operations. We're going to start in three months, but right now I can't think about the best business model for EatLike.

My biggest problem was to tell my team that we had to stop operations – like I couldn't even tell them! I was honestly kind of embarrassed, but I told them. I just felt very bad that I couldn't promise my word. I definitely think it took a toll on me, no joke. I told so many people this idea about EatLike and we got so many investors and so many people involved in it and then I had to tell them we were pausing operations. To get so many people to believe in you and you can't deliver is the worst feeling ever. Dealing with that is not fun.

8. On a lighter note, what are some exciting opportunities that have come from YouTube?

>YouTube has definitely brought a lot. Now, I basically work with YouTube and build features for them. I get to know what's going on algorithm-wise, I get to know the YouTube team very well, I get to visit their headquarters. You just know the platform better. Unlike any other platforms, YouTube really cares about their creators. Being a YouTuber has allowed me to make better videos with a better team.

9. What is your foremost advice to teen entrepreneurs?

>You have to believe in yourself way before you get started. If you're looking for an answer or approval from someone else, it's impossible. You need to believe in yourself so much, because people are going to bring you down.

10. What is your advice to teenagers that want to build their business or brand from social media?

>Use TikTok to boost your YouTube or Instagram. You need to reach people before they become your customer. You have to build trust with people before they start paying you money. Therefore, you can work for so long without any payoff, but that's part of it.

>It's very normal to get absolutely nothing, but you earn people's trust and admiration – and that's enough. How do you earn people's trust? Well, I think it starts with being consistent. If I could give you any feedback, it would be pick 100 posts and then complain. Make 100 posts before you even judge your progress. Confidence comes from result and result only comes from doing the work. You will need to go through the motions first before you see the results to get the

confidence. From there, remind yourself that you need to earn people's trust before you earn a single dime.

7

Brennan Agranoff:

CEO and Founder of HoopSwagg

"It was not like I jumped from this kid in a garage to a million-dollar company. That was a four to five-year period of me working really hard behind the scenes."

Brennan is the CEO and founder of a custom athletic sock startup called HoopSwagg, which he began at the age of 13. Today, HoopSwagg has an annual revenue of more than $2 million dollars. Brennan has been featured in The New York Times, CNN, and US News. As a firm believer in problem-solving and hard work, Brennan shares his entrepreneurship journey and provides insight into everything HoopSwagg.

1. What prompted you to start your business, HoopSwagg?

    I grew up in Portland and my parents worked in Nike. They released these socks called Nike Lead socks and they had these blocks on the back and for whatever reason they were super popular. Everyone was wearing them, but they only had four basic colors. I was the kid that wanted to wear something different, so I basically figured out how to customize them.

    This took about six months of research. After that, I proved the concept, I started selling on my eBay, and that was when it turned into a real business. I've been selling stuff on eBay since I was seven, but I've always really loved the entrepreneurship side.

2. What is the purpose behind HoopSwagg?

For me, my business is more of a vehicle to learn things rather than something to make money from. It's more useful for me to meet people in unique situations and run into problems and problem solve, because learning all those things in context of a business is so valuable.

3. What was the process of launching and running HoopSwagg?

I had to start doing social media marketing off Instagram. I had no idea what I was doing – it was all trial and error. I had to learn how to make a website, what's customer support, how do you ship a package, how do you hire someone... I had to work through all of these confusing little things.

At the beginning, it was really slow growth – during my first year, we sold $10,000 dollars on eBay. It was not like I jumped from this kid in a garage to a million-dollar company. That was a four to five-year period of me working really hard behind the scenes.

By the time I was seventeen, I acquired a company. That led into a whole press of extravaganza where we landed on the front page of CNN and then basically every news outlet covered us. We moved into new manufacturing space. I've rented two to three warehouses now and we have around 20 employees.

4. What are some of the struggles you encountered along the way?

Obviously, there was the age thing – I was in high school. How do you balance social life? I played sports and I had to get good grades and also trying to run a company on the side.

One of my biggest struggles was hiring people. A lot of people have the context of working in a company and I never got that, because I never did work in a company. So, understanding how Human Resources works, how you hire employees, how do you give them the training they need to be successful, how do you build a company culture – these are all things that there isn't a checklist for.

There's nothing necessarily out there that tells you that you need to know these things – you only figure them out once you screw them up. Learning what I don't know and figuring out what I don't know before it affects my company. There's always going to be problems in a company, but it's about how good you are at solving them.

5. How did you find opportunities to travel the world through the success of your business?

I started to get asked to speak at marketing conferences. I started doing more outreach and connecting with other kids who also spoke at conferences. I was building my network.

There's something that needs to be said about building relationships in person, and that was my excuse to go traveling and meet new people and experience new things. There's so much freedom at the age between sixteen to twenty-two that you'd be crazy to not take advantage of it.

Again, on creating opportunities for yourself – one of my best friends that I found through an online competition. He's incredibly talented at film. So, I started a creative agency where he manages the creative aspect of it and I basically source all the deals. The agency, which is called UnFilmed, shoots ads for e-commerce companies.

6. Why should teenagers start their own business?

I think that starting a business is the most useful thing you can do. Not because of the money – I can expect to make no money, but because you can learn a lot of things and meet a lot of people. You figure out a lot about yourself, including what you like, what you don't like, are you good at this, are you not good at this, and who do you get along with.

I remember going to high school and it's really easy to get trapped in your own crowd that you don't realize you're not moving outside of that. There are so many people that you become friends with that will open your mind and I see business as a way to create meaningful relationships as well as teach yourself things.

4
People, People, People

*I am currently a student...
but how can school prepare me for my future career?*

The truth is that you are not the equivalent of a successful 50-year-old who has six different business and a fortune under his thumb. I'm going to predict that you're still in school and you're a student. Use these years of your life to set a firm foundation for yourself: a beginning full of ingenuity, connectivity, and new experiences.

1 Meaningful Connections: Honesty

It's crucial to learn how to make friends with people that will have your back no matter what – in high school and every business industry. While you should always take up the opportunity to talk to or learn from talented or unique individuals, your focus should be building friendships and connections with people that you can depend on. Who are the people that will lend you help and loan you money when your business is crippling? Who are the people that give you brutally honest advice (even though you may not want to hear it) to make your business better? The people in your inner circle should be people that are not afraid to tell you the truth about yourself and your business.

Although these people may not be the most talented or the most intellectual individuals, these people will be the ones that give you honest advice and support no matter what.

2 Learning Connections: The Staircase Method

In high school, being the most popular person won't guarantee you a successful career or lifestyle. High school is merely a stepping stone, and every learning environment has smart people or talented individuals that you can learn from.

The staircase method is an essential concept to make mutual beneficial connections in order for you to expand your knowledge and skill set.

Visualize a staircase. You meet a Spanish-speaker, and you learn Spanish from them. Acquiring the skill of speaking Spanish helps you onto the first step of the staircase. You meet a digital designer, and you learn how to create 3D filters to promote your new brand on Instagram or Snapchat. Second level of the staircase. Based on the staircase concept, this keeps going as you continue to learn and continue to develop new skills from diverse people.

The best thing about the staircase is that it is endless. There is no end to learning and no end to acquiring new skills. If you understand the concept of the staircase now, hopefully it can start motivating you to get ahead of the game and start connecting with people that will help you climb those stairs.

Who Do You Choose To Connect With?

Go out of your way to get to know as many people as possible, so that you can interact with people from all backgrounds and personalities.

In high school, individuals that are more open to talking with their peers, teachers, and alumni can be able to understand a bit about their lifestyle and how it differs from yours. In business, CEOs are always observing people; they determine and differentiate which connections can be long-lasting and strong as well as which connections can help them learn new things.

So, be observant about everything from the way that different individuals act, the way that they speak, and down to the way that they move. In my sophomore year of high school, I had a senior friend (who eventually got into the Parsons School of Design in New York) that I would constantly observe. Despite the fact that she wasn't the A+ student, she had incredible personality traits and it affected the people around her. Her easy and charismatic demeanor was one of the things that my style of leadership lacked — and something that I knew I wanted to learn and employ.

Throughout your school years, you are exposed to a diverse group of students. Learn from people that have the skills that you don't possess, people that put in the work to pursue their goals, and people that have qualities that you admire. Be open about where you are lacking in skill or knowledge and ask for advice from the people that have deeper knowledge about a certain topic. If you can do anything in high school, it's to do your best to learn from the people around you instead of just sticking your head in a pile of textbooks hour after hour.

A Glimpse Into How Businesspeople Formulate Mutually Beneficial Relationships

The business industry is another case of building your network and your learning connections. Through your career, you will meet a ton of people that are experts in their fields. Always take up an opportunity to talk to them and learn from them.

Tip 1
Observe Your Potential "Learning Connections"

Businesspeople have to pay attention to the things that their associates are discussing during non-business settings, which include karaoke rooms, bars, lounges, dinners, and more. Topics discussed can include investment, technology, AI, politics, companies, and important names in the industry to family, sports, cars, fashion trends, celebrity friends, or gossip.

All in one, be open to learning about and discussing a wide range of topics. The point is that if you encounter a topic that you have almost no idea about, ask the other person to tell you more about it. Share their knowledge, and you have the chance to pick their brain. Valuing someone else's intelligence is a big compliment. Not only will you be able to learn something entirely new, you can also give someone else a chance to be in charge of the conversation.

Always maintain a good balance of how much you talk and how much the other person talks, so that both of you can learn from each other's ideas and expertise.

Tip 2

If They Don't Like You, They Won't Do Business With You

Doing business is not always based on one or two meetings – it is a relationship that takes time and effort. People don't do business with people they don't like. No matter how great your product/service is, the relationships and business connections that you formulate will set the tone for the success of your business. Tip 3 What To Expect Out of Snotty Attitudes, Arrogant Personalities, or Traditional Thinkers. Here is your guide for who NOT to work with in business.

A) First off, the "Snotty" attitude person is often easy to identify. They believe that everything they do and own is better than what you have, and that you should practically thank them for existing. Worst case scenario, they are rich as hell. They believe that their wealth and luxurious lifestyle immediately puts a barrier between you two; they want you to recognize that they are more superior than you and won't accept any signs of disrespect otherwise.

B) Secondly, the "Arrogant" personality individual is not the easiest person to have a clear communicative relationship with. You are constantly confused about whether or not your business deal has just ended, or if they have just implied something else with the way they expressed their arrogance. Either way, it's a headache of a situation when you are dealing with someone that has a temper tantrum every five minutes. These kinds of people are known for their loud bursts of anger, and you definitely will not want to be the subject of that anger's attack.

C) Lastly, the "Traditional" thinker might be one of the most difficult for Gen Zers to deal with. Traditionals often have totally polar mindsets, beliefs and business operation methods from Gen Zers. My biggest advice is patience and listening. Sometimes, the elder and more traditional businesspeople just want you to hear them out. Some people just might not understand WHY things operate the way they do today, since there has certainly been a digital conversion to online businesses over the last decade. To talk to them, try to visualize their thought process behind a conclusion or an ideology. When you are trying to negotiate for a way to solve a problem, don't force the "Traditional" thinker to think a certain way. Look at the situation from their perspective, and then kindly offer your take and politely explain your stance on why your personal take can also be helpful.

How Do You Keep in Contact With People?

As someone who has always been a part of a diverse and international community, people will come and go. Nevertheless, keeping and maintaining connections is more possible through social media in today's age.

1

Keep an eye out for their social media posts and updates.

A friend from high school (who is now a professional pianist) just posted an engagement photo on her Instagram page; be the first to congratulate her personally on the engagement.

2

Ask for their contacts,

and utter the phrase: "Let's keep in contact. If you need a favor, I'm only a text message or call away." While having 6,000 contacts is unnecessary, it is important to reach out to people and exchange contact information with people that you've found interesting to be around, so you can keep in touch.

3

Get-togethers,

such as parties or drinks, or even video calls with people far away can help you connect and reconnect with a lot of different people. This can also be an opportunity for you to branch out to other networks and individuals, while maintaining your current connections.

4

Present gifts or small tokens of your gratitude.

A wrapped gift near the holiday season can always can also leave a good impression. Therefore, people are more likely to sense how deeply you value this relationship.

Why Do You Want To Keep In Contact With People?

The million-dollar question. When you are in the midst of social circles and meeting different people in high school or university, this is the chance to learn from people of diverse backgrounds, ethnicities, skill sets, and experiences.

Building a network of people, especially those that you have formed strong connections with over the years, can be useful to you in the future if you ever bump into an obstacle where you need emotional, physical or financial help.

Of course, keep in mind that these relationships will also require sacrifice and support from you to them too. Don't take relationships for granted and always return favors.

3 How You Interact With Others = Who You Are

Here is something that you should drill into your brain: you are defined not only by your personal characterization of who you are, but also the way you interact with other people and how you react to different situations, especially crises.

People don't completely define you, but the way that you socialize will definitely put you into a categorical box within society.

Why is social interaction so important?

Learning how to determine, analyze, and communicate with every type of person is a strong skill in business relationships. To deconstruct the different types of business figurines, take a look at these examples:

1 Outspoken & Opinionated

You have a lot of your own ideas, and you constantly deliver A+ pitches. Always seeking the next challenge and unlikely to give up. Some individuals in this category may show signs of stubbornness or a hot-headed temper.

2 Problem-Solving & Clear Analysis

Assertive attitude and confidence can indicate that you are built for an intense work culture, filled with constant problems appearing here and there, while also receiving immense pressure from competitors, employers, colleagues, or clients.

3 People-Person & Social Butterfly

Work extremely well with others and they tend to like you immediately. You don't usually get into heated arguments, and you prefer to negotiate your way out of problems. Communication is a key aspect of your work philosophy.

After reading through these common leadership personas, I want to stress that one leader can possess more than one of these characteristics. To have all three or a perfect balance of all three will not necessarily equal the ideal leadership type, but individuals should always pursue to learn the positive sides of these personas.

4 Walking Down A Wrong Path In High School – Is It Too Late?

It's never too late to start over again. A lot of people don't even begin to deal with the fact that the people around them have been dragging them down and negatively influencing them for quite a while. In the back of their minds, they aren't too worried about bad influences, because you've got to have fun while you're young, right?

To some extent, that's true. But it's not true enough to make you not regret the time you lost throughout your adolescence, where you could have been doing something great – such as writing a book or getting a job.

If you know that you've fallen down the deep end, so my advice is to get out of there as fast as you can and don't look back. Thank your bad relationships for making you realize that you don't want to be treated badly… thank your bad friends for helping you hit rock bottom, so you can finally understand what it feels like to get back up on your feet AND be on your own… and thank yourself for making bad decisions – so you have the power to make better ones in the future.

5
Social Media + Gen Z

I am an Instagram, YouTube, Twitter, Pinterest, TikTok, or SnapChat user, but how do you make money off social media?

"The will to create is encoded in human DNA."

– Reid Hoffman, co-founder of LinkedIn

Remind me of social media's core purpose? Oh right – content creation and creative freedom at its best.

Surrounded by all the books that give you a step-by-step breakdown of how to become the next social media darlin' or provide strategies into making money off social media platforms, people forget that social media is something really fun.

If you take a look from 18-year-old YouTuber Emma Chamberlain to 15-year-old TikTok star Charli D'Amelio, they were never eyeballing their growth analytics or trying to crack the algorithm. They simply did what they truly loved to do – create authentic content – and other people responded.

I'm not saying that you should "keep making content and you'll eventually blow up." I'm stressing the fact that social media is not all about the follower count, subscriber count, or the number of likes or views you get on each post. It's about creating consistent, quality content that is enjoyable for both you and your audience.

So, step one is to make quality content. Step two – which I will proudly introduce you to – is how to obtain more credibility and eventually be able to grow your own online empire – and there are many ways to do this with and without worrying about a follower count.

What's The Difference Between

A Social Media *FOLLOWING* and a Social Media *AUDIENCE*?

Creating an audience is not the same as making "connections," because social media is a virtual society and you're not necessarily looking to make MILLIONS of friends. Your audience is supposed to be a group of people that simply enjoy the content that you create, and follow along your journey, whether it be the process of running a business or going on a European trip.

You want to develop a loyal following, and you won't be able to buy a bunch of followers off of some virus-plagued website to do that. Trust me, I've done the whole shebang.

The people that actually "blow up" on social media will not be someone that posts one good piece of content. Not everyone can blow up in a day, AND be able to keep up their internet fame for a long period of time.

A lot of people that get one good video to go viral on YouTube won't have the same results the next time they post another video. Every piece of content is different, and the results that you get won't always be the same. This is why you should NEVER focus on the idea of gaining the number of followers, but the quality of each and every follower in order to eventually turn those followers into potential future customers/clients.

How Can You Make Social Media A Source of Revenue?

I Have A Social Media Audience (>10K)

The larger the social media audience, the more likely that you can generate revenue off of a social media platform. Here are a few options that you can consider to make money from platforms such as TikTok, Instagram, Snapchat, and YouTube.

- Ambassador Program:

Businesses, especially brands that want to promote their products, will contact you (or vice versa, you can contact them to better understand their ambassador program) about becoming an ambassador or joining their ambassador program.

An ambassador program helps brands utilize influencers to promote their product/service, their brand message, or their brand in general. In return for being an ambassador and promoting their brand, the brand might return the favor by 1) giving the influencer a discount for purchasing their products 2) inviting the influencer to join an exclusive VIP group (the VIP group might distribute special party invites, limited edition products, etc.), or 3) paying you a certain amount of money.

Brand Deals (sponsored posts, influencer marketing, etc.):

You often hear your favorite influencers promote a product through their social media along with a caption and #ad or #sponsored. Brands pay influencers to do sponsored posts in order to drive sales, increase visibility, and reach more potential customers through the influencer's social media audience. According to Allure, social media influencer/reality television celebrity Kylie Jenner makes $1.2 dollars for every sponsored Instagram post.

Most brands pay influencers a retainer basis (upfront payment) of approximately $300 for a sponsored post, but it depends on the size of your social media audience (e.g. A-list celebrity with 1.1 million followers, blogger with 250,000 monthly viewers, podcaster with 15,000 listeners, YouTuber with 20,000 subscribers), the industry that you are in, the engagement of your audience, etc.

Through social media platforms like TikTok, the influencer has about 15 seconds to promote a product and capture their audience's attention. As long as the influencer meets the requirements that the brand has set – tagging the brand's TikTok account, for instance – they can make revenue through these brand deals.

Growing and Selling Accounts:

Businesses don't want to go through the tedious process of starting their own social media account and growing their audience step-by-step. They would prefer if someone else (you) has already done the heavy-lifting of audience-growing for them.

You can start a social media account that is fixed in a specific niche and begin growing a target audience. Once you reach 10K or a good amount of followers in a specific niche, you can sell that account to an ideal customer.

Affiliate Marketing:

Affiliate marketing is promoting a brand or an individual's products, while attaching your discount code ("use code KATE for a 20% discount off all items") or link. If an individual from your social media audience uses your discount code or link to buy an item, then you will be paid a certain percentage per sale that you make.

Amazon offers an affiliate program where influencers can buy products that they think their audience will like. As soon as someone buys the item using the influencer's provided link, they can receive a commission for every purchase made by their social media audience. If you see the 'Swipe Up' feature on Instagram or Snapchat and the influencer is linking her aesthetic nightstand from Amazon, it can be a form of revenue through Amazon's affiliate program.

YouTube Partnership Program (YPP):

To start making money off of YouTube, you need to apply for the YouTube Partnership Program (YPP) and get accepted. Qualifications for acceptance into the YPP include a minimum of 1,000 subscribers and at least 4,000 public watch hours in the span of the last 12 months. YouTube pays attention to your watch time or audience retention, because they want your videos to capture people's attention and therefore stay on their app for a longer period of time. After your channel is reviewed and accepted into the YPP, you're able to make revenue with ads, YouTube premium subscribers, and channel membership. Furthermore, you get access to special features, including SuperChat and an option to sell your merchandise.

Monetizing your channel means that you can gain revenue per video depending on the number of views you receive. On average, YouTubers get $1 dollar for every 1,000 views. Ultimately, the YPP is the top choice for any YouTuber who wants to turn their number of views into a higher number on their bank account.

Live Streams aka Donations:

Live streaming on TikTok can be a fast source of revenue for TikTok influencers. In the TikTok app, you can purchase coins, which is in-app currency that converts to real money. For instance, the App Store will have you confirm a $1.39 dollar purchase for getting 100 coins on TikTok. Those coins can be used to buy gifts (a 'drama queen' is worth up to $52.68 dollars or 5,000 coins), which you can give to influencers when they go on a live stream. The influencer can then collect his/her 'gifts' from her TikTok audience and convert those into diamonds, which can later transfer into real cash via PayPal.

If you already have at least 1,000 followers, TikTok allows you to do live-streaming with your fans. You can use the live streaming opportunity to connect with your audience and earn some revenue through these donations.

Shopping Cart (Dou Yin):

The Chinese version of the TikTok app, Dou Yin, has a special shopping cart feature where influencers can sell their products to their audience during a live stream. The purchasing process is easy and the shopping cart is a great way for influencers to promote their own brand products or do a sponsored ad.

Merchandise:

Influencers can create their own brand with their merchandise (or merch) through social media platforms. Instagram and YouTube are popular platforms for influencers to promote their merch, because they can drive traffic towards the shop on the main website. Take David Dobrik's merchandise collection for instance. He creates new collections (ClickBait, David's Disposables, etc.) featuring mugs, hoodies, iPhone cases, and even picture calendars. In his YouTube videos and Instagram promotional posts, his strategy of getting the entire Vlog Squad to wear his merch invigorates his social media audience to also want to buy the merch. Then, his audience can easily click on a link or a 'Swipe Up' that takes them to the FanJoy website, where they can purchase different items from David's merch collections.

I Do Not Have A Social Media Audience (<10K)

Not everyone can be an influencer, but there are other ways to tap into the income stream through social media platforms.

Social Media Marketing Agency (SMMA):

A SMMA provides services such as social media marketing, social media management, content creation, running ads, and social media consulting. This is a popular choice for many teenage entrepreneurs, because there isn't a resume attached to starting your own SMMA and it can be run by anyone with any level of experience in social media marketing. All you need is your phone and WiFi to start your SMMA.

You can charge however much you want, but the pricing for your services has to be an amount that your client can be able to pay. It also needs to be realistic – you can't expect clients to pay you a monthly retainer of $1,500 dollars if you have little to no experience with social media marketing. On average, a beginner SMMA can charge their clients $300 dollars per month. An expert (or someone who has been running their own SMMA for one or two years and have delivered positive results to their clients) can charge their clients with up to $3,000 dollars per month for their services.

Coaching:

Coaching on social media can allow you to distribute your knowledge towards your clients, and you can make money through virtual coaching sessions. Your first step is narrowing down your niche and contacting potential clients in the same niche.

Let's say that you are a personal fitness trainer. You've contacted 100 people on Instagram about your services. Start by offering a free 10 minute video call with a potential client that is interested in your fitness services and conduct a personalized training session. After that, you can offer more fitness coaching video calls with $70 dollars for a 30 minute time slot. If your clients see positive results from your fitness coaching services, you can bump up the pricing for your one-on-one fitness coaching services later on.

Webinars/Online Class Programs:

You often find these gurus talking about 'how to travel the world without having to do the 9-to-5 job' or 'how to dominate the TikTok algorithm in 10 days.' These so-called gurus have built up their experience in a certain topic and would offer a program of 20 videos or so to teach you on whatever they are good at. The point is – you can do it too!

Set up your own online class or program through a website like Skillshare.com, shoot a couple of videos, create a mesmerizing trailer that captures what your program is all about, put your trailer on social media ads, pull in those customers, and you're ready to go.

Do Free Stuff:

Nobody will know who you are when you begin your business. You can start gaining basic experience in your business's niche by contacting potential clients who are in need of your services.

For a social media marketing agency, contact 100 people on Instagram per week. You get 30 responses, and 10 people that are willing for you to manage their social media business account for one month for FREE. After one month, you can request a referral (ask the person to share your work with ten of their friends) from that client so that you can gain more visibility and get more people to know about your services. Later on, you can start charging people as you build up your experience and you get better at what you are doing.

The main point of doing free stuff is to build up on your experience; in order for you to gain credibility and be able to charge your clients more, you will need to have a firm background of experience in your expertise.

Everything You Need To Know About Target Audience

A target audience for a social media account/business/influencer will be the people that are going to hype up your collection drops, inquire about your brand, and be engaged in your social media content. The more specific the target audience – the better. Eventually, your target audience can be transferred into actual customers or clients with an interest in your brand.

Knowing your target audience can help you decide when to launch your products, what your potential customers are looking for, who your potential clients are, etc. In the analytics feature for the business account on Instagram, users can understand more information about their target audience.

Who is your target audience – a single stay-at-home mother or a Wall Street businessman? What is your target audience looking for (skincare companies might create a poll to ask their audience if they want a mist spray or a smoothing cream)? What is the age group, ethnicity, or country of your target audience? When do they check their social media platforms? What is a good time to post important content if you have an international audience? Do you want to engage with social media accounts in a specific niche?

Businesses want to know more about your target audience, because their target audience = their potential customers.

You want adapt your product/service to fit the wants and needs of your customers. Collecting information on your target audience through analytics can allow you to better decide how to move forward with your business and what new changes you want to implement.

The Golden Rule of Social Media Trafficking

Teenagers can easily go viral in less than two weeks with a dancing video on TikTok. But if you are trying to grow your brand and connect with your audience through Instagram DM, you want to link your Instagram handle in your TikTok profile.

Trafficking your audience from one platform to the next can help you grow your audience in different platforms, or platforms where you want to grow your business. Linking your other social media profiles can allow your audience to connect with you on social media platforms that they are more familiar with.

For instance, photographer/internet personality Bryant Eslava is known for creating SnapChat and Instagram filters for his social media audience. Since Instagram takes a longer time to confirm his filters compared to SnapChat, he would ask his audience to 'Swipe Up' and subscribe to his SnapChat account in order to unlock all his filters. Through this trafficking method, he opens another doorway for his 5.5 million followers to better connect with him and build hype around each filter release.

How To Market Your Own Business On Social Media
1 Let's Talk About the "Hype" Strategy

Setting a tone of exclusivity and a brand of uniqueness will go a long way for the future of your business. One industry that has earned millions from the past decade has mastered one perfect strategy on selling its products.

Hypebeast, Off-White, and Yeezy's are some of the biggest names in the fashion industry, targeting millennials and Gen Zers. Each collection drop, whether it is for a particular fashion season or a holiday line, holds a reputation of exclusivity. With the limited amounts of stock from each collection, people are not worried about how high the price is when they click the Buy Item button on the check out website. In today's generation, people want to buy something that you can't get from the nearby Walmart or the closest shopping mall. They want to grab ahold of Kanye West's limited edition Yeezy's or the new Kylie Jenner lip kits that sold out in less than a day.

YouTuber Eva Gutowski's architectural design brand, It's All Wild, launched a new collection in March 2020. Within moments of launching items for purchase on the brand's website, a lot of them were selling out in minutes. How did she manage to get people to buy her products so quickly — and with her audience responding with such a high level of eagerness?

AMBIGUITY OF BRAND

Eva would post a photo of herself wearing a red off-shoulder crop top, tagging her brand's Instagram account, @itsallwild. This same pattern occurred for a few months, as she also dropped hints of her 'coding a website' or posting a Photoshop design of prints on her Instagram stories.

She never elaborated on her brand specifically or gave away a lot of information. Her tactic promoted conversations in her comments section, where her followers would each make their own suggestions and interpretations on the upcoming brand — as social media often does. Without acknowledging her brand in a straightforward explanation or outline, people were anticipating to find out more about Eva's new collection and the unique pieces that were going to be sold.

REPOSTS, SHARES, & WORD OF MOUTH

Eva is a style icon of our age as she dabbled in YouTube, film photography, and channeled our teenage fantasies of taking a detour stay in Hawaii. Her content has generated an audience, and unknowingly (to the audience), that audience has transformed into clients that can fuel her revenue and a business through social media. Hours before her new collection launched, she reposted photos from her fans, featuring an It's All Wild photoshoot and a few clothing pieces.

Since a lot of people wanted to have their account show up on Eva's Instagram story (with 7.5 million followers, she was bound to receive a lot of social media engagement), they would repost or share her It's All Wild-related photos.

Whether individuals were seeking to be possibly featured to Eva's large Instagram audience or simply a fan of her, these reposts and shares were important to spreading the word on Eva's new collection launch.

CELEBRITIES OR INFLUENCERS

When a social media influencer (like Eva) or a well-known celebrity reposts a pair of designer shoes on Instagram or tweets about a new collection drop on Twitter, it instinctively triggers you to get to know the company or source. Why? Because you want to know WHY this influencer or celebrity is promoting or talking about this company.

You flip open their website at the link in bio, you check out other items from their online shop, and you continue to scroll and scroll. People are storming through the doors of the pop-up shop in L.A or being the first ones in front of their computer, fingers lingering over the purchasing page as soon as companies drop a long-awaited collection. All thanks to the massive audience of celebrities and influencers, which allows them to make money off a paid promotion or sponsored post, this new frontier of social media marketing has attracted millions of companies to turn a traditional culture into digital one.

Secondly, the fact is that I don't know every single celebrity on the planet, but I do know a few. This is where *collaborations* take on their own spin of social media marketing. Before creating her own brand, YouTuber Eva Gutowski collaborated with Colourpop Cosmetics, which introduced Colourpop to Eva's audience and vice versa. Collaborating with another social media influencer or a celebrity can allow exposure to a wider audience and the opportunity to connect with different people in different industries.

CONCLUSION

Limited edition brands offer limited supplies for a high price, attracting customers' attention. Although some may argue that the "hype" of a brand is unnecessary, this tactic works like a charm according to a few millionaires.

2 Enhancing VIP Customer Experience

Your customers are impatient creatures that can hit the unsubscribe button to your email list or unfollow you on all the socials in less than a minute. You DO NOT want to lose or upset your customers – especially those that spend a lot of money buying your business's products/services.

VIP EVENTS

Go ahead – plan and host a VIP event to court your devoted (and profitable) customers.

A well-planned event will go a long way for your customers, and they will likely leave with a (hopefully positive) impression of your company. In other words, VIP events will allow you to develop a highly-respected reputation, where your customers can feel like they are part of an exclusive community. Below is an example.

1) Consider a fancy dress-up dinner party at a nearby restaurant if you are celebrating the launch of your Halloween clothing collection.
2) Be aware of your invite list and how each person invited can possibly benefit your brand in the short term or long term, such as potential clients or important customers. A rule of thumb is to never invite two competitors, because you don't want your business to be in the center of an uncomfortable or perhaps even troublesome conflict.

> NOTE: designing digital posters or broadly sharing information to the public about this party is not necessary – you want exclusive parties to promote itself through attendees' social media or word of mouth.

3) Invite celebrities or influencers (if you can) to **increase your brand's social media presence and promote the exclusivity of this party.**
4) Hire a professional party-planner or assign someone to manage all aspects of the party, including things that might go wrong.
5) Provide upgrades, secret access to a private lounge, or any other additions that might make VIPs feel like they are spending their money in the right way.
6) Socialize and be present if you are the CEO of the company. Otherwise as an employee or intern, do your assigned job – learn to observe and look out for important people that can take you up the social ladder, so you can find an opportunity to strike up a conversation sometime during the course of the party.
7) Execute professionally and ensure that everything goes as planned. A good party earns you a good reputation that might make your company name end up at the top of social media headlines. On the contrary, a party that has a few notable mishaps or a fistfight in the middle of the dance floor can earn a poor reputation that might brand your company negatively on social media forever. Either way, you'll receive some level of exposure with this social media marketing strategy. The only difference is how you want your company to remembered. Take some time to think about it.
8) Lastly, your VIP events have to be an experience that will be memorable for your VIPs. Don't let it fall under the traditional guidelines and don't even walk close to a party handbook.

SOCIAL MEDIA VIP GROUPS

Say that you've built a highly-renowned reputation in an industry or have established a business – utilize your social media platforms to take that next level of exclusivity for your customers.

An important detail that you have to first realize is that you have to understand what type of culture, tone, niche, and audience you are targeting. Whilst retail fashion brands prefer to involve everyone, a women's writing club may only invite published female authors, bloggers, freelancer writers, and a few additional aspiring writers. Review how these social media marketing tactics, especially regarding the VIP stance, and how it will contribute to your overall reputation as a business.

INSTAGRAM 'CLOSE FRIENDS'

In 2018, Instagram launched the 'close friends' feature for their Instagram stories. 'Close friends' allowed people to select certain people that could view their stories… soon enough, online entrepreneurs found a profitable spin to Instagram's new feature.

Once you create a reputation or establish an audience that is curious, inquisitive, or interested in constantly understanding more about you or your business, you can begin crafting out who is going to be on your list.

After posting to your Instagram story about the exclusive spots offered in your VIP 'close friends' list, begin writing down potential offers, such as discount codes, private party invites, sneak-peaks, exclusive behind-the-scenes, Instagram takeovers with public figures, Q&A sessions where Instagram influencers spill the beans on their success, rare footage depending on your niche/industry, and more. Your DMs will be flooded with questions and requests to join the invite list as soon as you post about what your VIP 'close friends' list offers.

Now, you are not making a VIP 'close friends' list for nothing if not to make a bit of cash. Ask your potential applicants to either email or DM you an application, and charge a one-time entry fee for you to review the application. If a person goes through the enrollment process and makes it into the VIP 'close friends' list, ensure that they pay a monthly or annual fee to keep their spot in the list. Offer refunds if you can and make sure that your VIP content lives up to expectations.

FACEBOOK GROUPS

One of my top-recommended Facebook groups is Ghost Gang, created by entrepreneur and social media influencer India Severe aka Indy Blue aka a lesser-known Kylie Jenner. Her "I love you say it back" motto attracted hundreds of thousands of people, birthed the Lonely Ghost brand, and her Ghost Gang Facebook group continues to be a lively outlet for anyone to express their feelings, their thoughts, their opinions, their creativity, and be able to meet and connect with one another.

Many Facebook groups have a short application process with approximately five questions that is later reviewed by the admin(s). This is the part where you can either set the tone for an exclusive culture or an everyone-is-welcome culture depending on your niche.

Although I don't suggest earning cash up-front, there are other ways to grow your business through Facebook groups.

Facebook's policies and features change constantly, which is important to transfer your Facebook group members into <u>long-term email subscribers</u>. Communicating with a large audience is easy in Facebook groups, and you can easily connect with potential customers or clients that agree to join your mailing list.

Sponsors or advertisers can also be seeking a tight-knit community or a specific target audience. Maintain a high profile and reputation within your community; spams or irritating self-promotion such as 'follow my TikTok account' should not be allowed. Therefore, advertisers and sponsors will reach out to you with a request to feature or post an advertisement, promoting their product/service. This is where you have the power to charge a fee for advertisements (which will appear as links) to be posted within the group. Remember: don't overuse this tip, because your members definitely would not want to be bombarded with an excess of advertisements.

Finally, you want to be able to reach marketing managers and advertising companies to negotiate a deal about the pricing of one or more promotions/shout-outs. If your community is popular enough, it's vice versa – marketing managers and advertising companies will be quick to get in contact with you.

CRASH COURSE

<u>Long-Term Email Subscribers</u>

The thing is, I bet that more than half of the Gen Z population don't check their emails on a daily or weekly basis.

Usually, I sign up for an email newsletter from a brand's website, and I get weekly or even daily emails that remind me to check on their new items, join a webinar, etc. I'll be honest – I hate it. I discard hundreds each week and take too much time unsubscribing to newsletters than I am joining them. Every email is a blunt and an automated message designed to capture your attention and hook you to click on the website link, purchasing the company's product/service.

I've seen so many of these emails that I can basically recreate one of my own. My point is that I don't see anything new, fun, or even remotely creative.

Tip 1

Get To The Point and Get Out

I've seen so many entrepreneurs suggest that you create a dynamic and intriguing storyline that hooks your audience/potential client into the main point of your email newsletter. STOP THAT. Real businesspeople don't like flowery language and excessive small-talk – they want to get straight to the point.

In your email, get straight to your point with a visibly large headline, and describe the headline with a brief 1-2 sentences sub-headline. Add other details that are necessary, but remember that Gen Zers have an attention span of eight seconds. Images with bright colors, but would still coincide nicely with your website's color palette and your business's style. Then, most importantly, add a link to a website or a video or wherever you want your audience to end up at.

Tip 2

3D Posters + Videos Are Up For Game

The current generation is no longer fascinated by a digital photograph – they want something that is dynamic and captivating.

Online marketing needs to start shifting faster towards 3D posters made in Photoshop or Spark AR, animated and interactive graphics, or adapt more short videos to promote their businesses.

Time is what people want, people always want more time. This is why they might not spend more than 20 seconds looking at a boring video you made, whereas they can choose to do something else that they want to do. It's all about attention span, and holding onto a few more seconds of your audience's attention. Here is a breakdown of what your 3D posters or videos can look like:

0 - 7 seconds

is your business's name and the product/service you are promoting.

8 - 12 seconds

is dramatic and/or meaningful cinematography that extends onto your product/service.

13 - 20 seconds

is to get your message delivered to your audience 110%, leave a distinctive and significant impression in their minds, and WRAP IT UP!

Tip 3

Let's Future-Proof For A Second

Diving into the reality of email marketing can reveal the fact that a lot of people are READING their emails anymore. With smart-techs like Alexa or Google Pixel, you want your email to be clear, direct, and properly formatted.

Tip 4

Target The Right People Using Email Segmentation

Email marketing can be complex and may not always deliver the results that you expect. Sending the same email to one person may not invigorate them or interest them the same way that it does for the next person that opens your email.

This is why individuals should make use of email segmentation, which helps you separate your email subscribers into various smaller groups and can help you categorize them easily and decide what content best fits each group.

1. Engaged Potential Customers: spend the most time creating interactive marketing email for this pool of email subscribers. They are likely to become long-term customers or be extremely passionate in you or your company. Still, you want them to eventually end up at the purchasing page.
2. Opens-The-Email-Not-The-Link Group: give the general content to these people, but also be dedicated into formulating eye-catching

marketing content. You want to shape your email into a trap that leads straight to your link. These people may click your email and not care about you or your business at all, or perhaps they might briefly skim through the content. With these people, it's a step-by-step process. Your goal is to make your content engaging enough to the point where you've finally captured their attention, and hopefully move them up the notch to the first category.

3. "Ah, More Spam": send the unsubscribe email to them, suggesting that your content and business might not be right for them. If they don't unsubscribe, continue sending content, but much less. Consider monthly emails that summarizes new product/service launches or any other message that you want to address.

3 Go-To Social Media Marketing Tools

- Swipe-Up Feature: this feature takes Instagram story viewers directly to another website.
- Tagging Other Profiles: tagging another company, a business partner, your own business profile, or yourself can allow your social media audience to check out other (or your own) profiles.
- Create Filters: users can customize their own filters; many companies are creating their own Instagram or Snapchat filters to promote their products, since other users can simply tap the upper hand corner of the Instagram story to use the same filter themselves; Calvin Klein's CK Everyone Instagram filter attracted potential customers to their brand and to the launch of their new CK Everyone Fragrance.

Secrets To Success?

Two Words: Opportunity… and Luck

Did Charli D'Amelio work hard to establish her TikTok career? The answer is no, she never thought that she would be able to have such a huge social media audience and get the response that she did.

Hard work can definitely pay off sooner or later, but opportunity and luck can also come into play with success. Why are there instances where young content creators blow up on YouTube or go viral on TikTok? Is it their appearance or the quality of their content? Perhaps, but the most important thing is the the timing of opportunity.

I inquired a business management undergraduate (and friend), Richard Au, to explain the concept of opportunity and luck in the social media context. Here's what he had to say:

"For a person such as Charli D'Amelio, I'm sure she wasn't the very first TikTok user, but she capitalized on the TikTok trends at just the right time to become one of the most famous TikTok influencers out there. In a sense, she was lucky, because I'm sure there were thousands of other TikTok users when she was just beginning, but she came out on top.

"Why is it that the common argument is that the generation before us had it easier? Is it because they had simply more opportunities? Maybe, but they were born in a time where the entire world was changing in unprecedented ways, and opportunities arrive from those changes. They were lucky.

"In the day and age of technology, there are still tons of opportunities, but when millions of individuals are fighting on the same platform, hopping on the same trends, and doing the exact same things, how will top-notch quality bring you on top? It probably won't.

"In cases like this, you just need to be in the right time at the right moment with the right amount of luck. Even for YouTube.

"How do people gain millions of subscribers within months while others take a decade to get to 2 million? It's the matter of luck, opportunity, and timing. That aspect of businesses may be overlooked because it's something that people cannot necessarily control, but is super important. Some people are always so persistent on an idea because they believe that hard work may actually work. It does in most cases, but what if the timing simply wasn't right? Timing. Opportunity. Luck. You have to hop in at the right time, and if you're lucky, you might just hit the jackpot."

6
How To Pitch Yourself

*I interviewed for a job today,
but why didn't I GET the job?*

Never be the person that won't get a callback for an audition, gets rejected after an interview, or get your incredible skillset, personality, knowledge, and experience level OVERLOOKED by recruiters.

I've known a whole lot of people that have walked into a job interview and completely flunked it. As a student, I've seen students interview for a leadership position in a club and walk out the door without any sort of self-reassurance that they got the position. The worse kind is when individuals have no idea what they did wrong at all.

The icky get-go for job-hunting beginners can be a long and painful process – unemployed and sleeping on your friend's couch. The truth is if you know absolutely nothing about writing a resume, pitching yourself, or interview skills, you're not ready to even begin to apply for a job. I urge you to please… take it one step at a time.

STEP ONE: *How To Write a Resume*

A resume summarizes your skill set, accomplishments, and working experience as a whole. Hiring managers usually ask you to bring in your resume before or during an interview (a few interviewers have suggested that they won't even do an interview with someone if they didn't bring in their resumes, so have an extra copy of your resume prepared) in order for them to assess your capabilities on paper.

The point of a resume is to stand out of the crowd and explain to your hiring manager how your skills, knowledge, and experience can benefit their company. A company will not hire you if your resume is poorly written nor will they ask you to do the job interview (aka STEP TWO).

Here are all of the essentials that you need to add in a resume:

1/ CONTACT: super important! Remember to include your full name, email, address (if required), phone number, and social media handles (preferably LinkedIn and/or Instagram)

2/ OBJECTIVE: keep in mind (or you can include this in the Profile section) a clear goal about what you want to achieve if you get this job. DO NOT make your objectives self-focused, such as 'a great institution for *me* to gain more experience.' Alternatively, talk about how you can apply your skill set/experience to the company's benefit and how you can incorporate your ideas to help a department's team.

3/ PROFILE: short and simple, but to-the-point. Write one or three sentences that capture who you are as a professional in your industry. Hiring managers like to learn that you are motivated, a team player, organized, and dependable. Make sure to be direct and allow them to understand what your job is and what you are skilled. Give this part 110%, because a majority of hiring managers won't take more than 30 seconds to look at your resume before tossing it away and looking at the next one in the pile – a unique resume that proves that you are a qualified employee can grab a hiring manager's attention.

4/ EDUCATION: do not lie about your education, because the hiring manager can easily factcheck this or ask you a question about your education in the job interview. No abbreviation of school name allowed

and do not include your high school if you are currently enrolled in a college.
- Correct Example: The University of Pennsylvania
- Incorrect Example: UPenn

5/ SKILLS: list EVERYTHING that you can do from social media managing to portrait photography. Don't be afraid to put the most unexpected (but professional) skill items on the list, because you never know what job your employer will eventually ask you to do.

6/ EXPERIENCE: list ANY experience that you possibly have. Since most teenagers haven't done real-world jobs, they can still include fundraisers, events, clubs, or any leadership experience you've had in school (TIP: avoid mentioning the word 'school 'such as 'raised money for a school club, 'but instead try: 'raised 1,000 USD to donate to local school students that lacked learning resources.').
- *Higher Level*: volunteer work to provide resources for children in India; managed and organized a one-week pop-up shop for Brandy Melville in China which allowed the clothing brand to gain a Chinese audience.
- *Intermediate Level*: modeling for a television commercial for Pepsi; data analyzing at a local firm; freelance copywriting for international clients via UpWork.com.
- *Poor Level*: fundraising; organizing debate; grocery store employee.

7/ AWARDS/ACHIEVEMENTS: list ALL achievements or awards you have received. This part is not necessary in a resume, but it can prove your professional experience to the hiring manager that is reading your resume. Examples: 1st Place in LitMag Writing Competition for Short

Stories, First Place Winner of the University of California-Berkeley Business Startup Challenge, Winner of the Vogue Talent Content in 2015.

I suggest that before you write your resume, google "best resume examples" and you are guaranteed to find tons of professional examples. Mimic general key words from those resume examples to consider including into your own resume, but always keep it realistic to who you are.

After you complete your resume, I suggest that you have someone else check it over for 1) credibility, 2) professionalism, and 3) clear and neat formatting. You want the advice of someone who has had experience applying and getting jobs, because those individuals are likely to understand what your hiring manager is looking for and can pinpoint areas that you either need to change or improve in your resume.

In a school setting, you have to submit an application with various questions on who you are and why you think you are the perfect candidate for the job/position you are applying for. The common application questions include describing your leadership style, your vision for X club, your past achievements/experience in X club, how you are different compared to other candidates, and proposing a possible project/event idea for the following year. In other words, the questions on the applications are similar to what you want to outline in your resume.

<u>But what sets apart a FANTASTIC resume from an AWFUL resume?</u>

Tip 1

Grammar + A Good Deal of Professional Lingo

Have the human version of Grammarly (or insert it into the online Grammarly) do a sweep of your resume or application to check for errors or incorrect sentences. Then, take your resume to the next level by incorporating terms (they can be simple!) that apply to your job or the industry/company that you are or want to be working in. This professional lingo can allow hiring managers to notice your maturity and dedication into a resume in spite of being younger. Simple professional lingo words can be 'accomplished,' 'five years' experience,' 'in-depth knowledge,' 'strategic,' 'negotiation,' etc. It emphasizes your professional profile and how you can incorporate your abilities efficiently in their company.

Tip 2

Visual Presentation aka Be Neat

Neat as in organized, professional, and easy to read.

Your resume needs to be divided into sub-sections as listed above, including Experience and Skills. You will also need to attach a photo of yourself; there are no specific requirements for photo attachments, but just ensure that you're not putting a low-quality selfie or a picture of you holding a martini in a club wearing a crop top. Regarding formatting in general, hiring managers prefer a resume template with a sidebar, which separates your sections. In different resume templates, the sections of Contact, Profile, Education, Skills, Experience, and Awards/Achievements can be anywhere on the resume – you choose! As a general observation, I can only tell you that I've noticed that your name, image, and profession go on the very top of the resume. Your Profile usually goes up next on the main page and the Contact section is on the top of the sidebar. The rest follows below in either the main page or the sidebar.

Thankfully, your layout and templating skills in InDesign or Photoshop won't be necessary to craft your resume. What I suggest you do is search for resume templates online. Personally, I created a PDF resume via LinkedIn after inserting information into my LinkedIn profile, which can serve as a quick and easy way to formulate your own resume in a clear format.

Tip 3

In-Depth vs. Vague

As you have probably already read in the previous examples I've listed for the Experience section, the most basic rules of being in-depth include 1) explaining what the role was/what the job was and 2) how your job helped a company/a charity/a group/employees/other individuals.

The point is to not be lazy on your resume – or it may cost you a job opportunity!

Job Resume Exemplars:

"Managed and organized a one-week pop-up shop for Brandy Melville in China which allowed the clothing brand to gain a Chinese audience."

    Who: You, aka the manager of the pop-up shop

    What: Managed and organized a Brandy Melville pop-up shop

    When (e.g. time, setting, context): One week in China for Brandy Melville

    Who Does It Benefit: Promotes Brandy Melville's fashion brand to China customers

    What Does It Say About You?: Leadership, organization, management, and marketing skills. Experience with international sales.

"Fundraising."

This tells the hiring manager NOTHING about what your fundraising was about. This can cause the hiring manager to question if you had a random "fundraising" event where you cooked a plate of brownies and got 20 dollars for it or a "fundraising" event where you performed with your school band at the local carnival and raised 1,000 dollars for a nearby orphanage.

STEP TWO: *How To ACE A Job Interview*

The way to land your next (or possibly first) job is to dig yourself a pretty little tunnel to the interviewer's heart.

Before you walk out of the door, your goal is to leave your interviewer SHOCKED (in a good way), EXCITED (to learn more about you), and/or incredibly EAGER to give you the job on the spot (no need to anticipate a callback). Then, you'll be expecting one hell of a good report from the interviewer to your future boss.

Nevertheless, individuals often feel like they are being rudely interrogated by a superior. Why? Because your interviewer is asking tough questions, not smiling back, and they are basically what is standing between you and the job that you are applying for.

The truth is that this is probably the 21/45 interviews that your interviewer had to do today, and he/she is not looking forward to hearing the same boring and lame responses from every single interviewee. Your interviewer is bored, tired, and want something (or someone) that is out of the blue. So obviously, their professional and not-so-friendly attitude can make you feel stressed out.

In high school, students will begin to do some nerve-wracking real-world stuff, such as public speaking, talking to superiors or professionals, and most of all – sitting in a chair and basically being interrogated by an adult. I noticed that right before any high school student was about to do an interview with a university, a club, or any superior, they start shaking and begin to talk abnormally.

Here's a talking pattern that I want to share, and see for yourself if you fit into any of these categories: speak louder than normal, trip over their sentences, freeze up altogether at a question they don't understand, lower their speaking volume significantly, speed up, or chitter-chatter their teeth as if baby it's cold outside.

Anyways, let's convert all this nervousness into some numbers. In 2013, the Globe News Wire reported a survey that discovered that 92% of adults in the US get nervous during job interviews, along with 'having the jitters,' being late, being overqualified, being under qualified, being unprepared, and facing tough interview questions from the interviewer.

Not fun, heh?

It's important to know that if you are a part of the great-o majority 92 percentile, then that is totally normal. However, learning to ace a job interview means that you have to begin by eliminating your jitters.

How To Start Eliminating Your Jitters

I once walked out of an interview with my interviewer chasing quickly after me, continuing to flood me with questions on 1) how I was so self-reassured and calm, 2) if I regretted anything I said during the interview, 3) how I was able to answer every question without hesitation, 4) why I wasn't scared of my interviewers, and 5) why other people my age couldn't do a simple interview with the same level of confidence?

Q1: "How I Was So Self-Assured"

Self-assurance is not the act of being cocky, but it is the way you compose yourself in a confident manner as you are sitting in a chair and answering questions. Talking normally and conversationally is the key to presenting yourself as confident and self-assured.

Maintaining a calm mindset will get you through the interview quick and breezy. For me, I tried not to think about the fact that this interview was of VITAL IMPORTANCE and would literally determine if I got the job or not. Thinking too much will only result in sweaty palms and more jitters, which you don't want. Keeping the idea of the interview simple and conversational will help you seem more comfortable and will definitely make the entire process smoother.

As for a confident attitude, it's all about the way you present yourself in general. If your shoulders are slouched or you have bad posture, it can indicate to your interviewer that you're not prepared to pitch yourself – nor will you be able to talk in a meeting, collaborate with others, or handle a demanding job as a whole. If you're quiet or tone-deaf, that's an obvious sign that you're not ready to speak up to your superiors and you're not particularly communicative (which is a poor attribute for almost any applicant). If you cannot look your interviewer in the eye and respond to their questions, it clearly shows that you're not 100% assured in yourself or any possibility that you will land the job after this interview.

With a clearer mindset and holding yourself responsible to the way you present yourself to your interviewer, you can definitely pull off the 'self-assured' attitude in an instance.

Q2: "If I Regretted Anything I Said During the Interview"

My answer? No, I do not regret anything I said.

Why? Because I put my full trust in every word that I said in that interview, and I stand by every response to every question that I was asked.

After walking out of an interview, don't spend your time hovering over the things that you did wrong or that one response that could have cost you the job. DO NOT THINK ABOUT IT. Convince yourself that you did a great job and leave it at that.

Q3: "How I Was Able To Answer Every Question Without Hesitation"

If your interviewer has given you questions before the actual interview, take a quick skim of the questions and jot down a few ideas in your head. But, going overboard with writing down every question, writing an essay response to every question, and going the mile won't always benefit you during an interview.

I personally find it quite useful is to <u>not prepare too much</u>. Before you judge me about not preparing, let me explain. Overwhelming yourself with reviewing every possible interview question can be tiring and useless. This can also cause you to be hesitant as you try to gather the best responses to this question, review and compare them in your head, and before you know it your interviewer is already falling asleep.

Your interviewer wants to get to know YOU and YOUR ideas/opinions/thoughts, so practice thinking quickly and responding in a span of a second.

My strategy is that in response to an interview question, I would simply pick the first answer that comes to my head and say it out loud. Of course, be conscious of the quality of your response and how it resonates with the interviewers' expectations. This is so that you don't fuss over the question for too long, and you do not pull off the impression that you're hesitant or nervous. After you respond, try to think about as many ideas as possible to support your answer. Add on to WHY you think so in order for your interviewer to get a better glimpse of where you stand in your opinions. Then, your interviewer can analyze if your opinions (which is reflection of your personality and your performance in a work setting) match the job profile and the ideal person that the company wants to hire.

I once blurted out a response, which I ended up not 100% agreeing with after I gave it some thought and realized that it was a terrible idea. Still, I stuck to the first response and gave explanations, details, and even examples to support my answer. Challenge yourself to go with the flow during an interview, and see how you do. It will help you be more comfortable, so you don't feel the pressure of trying to memorize all your pre-planned responses at once.

Q4: "Why I Wasn't Scared of My Interviewers"

Getting intimidated by an interviewer will – no question – lower your interview performance. While a slight few do BETTER under rapid fire questions and pressure, most people crack like an egg as soon as they feel intimidated or interrogated in any way.

Start by eliminating that fear through regarding your interviewer like a friend. I'm not saying be super friendly and super comfortable; you want to maintain your professional appearance. However, remind yourself that your interviewer is there to get to know more about you. Talk about yourself, your ideas, the unique things that make you YOU, and especially how you can utilize your skill set and knowledge to benefit the company (or wherever you are applying to). And do it by talking normally, as you would to a friend or family member, to your interviewer.

People frequently forget that interviewers are also human, and they are not the rigid and professional personas 24/7. Therefore, you want your interviewer to be more comfortable around you and set aside their professional demeanor to talk to you in a less formal way. In some cases, you might end up talking to your interviewer about something completely off topic or your conversation might be very casual. Either way, your goal is to loosen up the tension to show that you are not afraid to be yourself and you are comfortable with meeting new people (an important skill to have for teamwork and leadership aspects during work).

If possible, make sure to get to know who your interviewer is before the actual interview. For example, during a college application process, the college alumni will contact you to get an interview. In a less creepy and less stalker-ish manner, check out the alumni's socials to get a sense of who you are going to be talking to. In addition, send a reply immediately after they reach out to you in order to show that you are present and engaged. Hence, you will feel more in control of the interview since you already have done a bit of background research into the interviewer and you'll be ready to go.

Q5: "Why Other People My Age (Teenagers) Couldn't Do A Simple Interview With The Same Level of Confidence?"

Every person of any age can accomplish all the things that I listed above: confidence over nervousness and self-assurance over hesitation. It all comes down to how well you control your mindset and how establishing one specific mindset can influence your interview performance.

I think the common misconception around teenagers not being able to ace an interview is due to the fact that they haven't done a lot of interviews in total. They don't know what to expect and they're not prepared for the questions, the interviewer, or the possibly pressure-cooker setting. My top advice is to be mentally prepared and be confident in how well you will do to an extent that you are able to sit at a chair and be more than fine with having interrogative questions thrown your way.

STEP THREE: *How To Pitch Yourself*

Pitching yourself is learning how to perfect the WHY ME argument before the interviewer loses interest or the hiring manager deletes your email application. Companies are constantly on the lookout for 'new blood,' which means recruiting people with fresh new ideas, thoughts, and opinions.

The Importance of: Why Me + The Unique Factor

In order to stand out of the crowd, your pitch needs to be about 1) why you are UNIQUE compared to other candidates, and 2) how you are able to implement your UNIQUE personality (which includes your important qualities and strengths) within the company.

An interview or a hiring process both have one thing in common – and it's the fact that they all end up being WIN-WIN situations. You land the job, and the company has a new employee that can take up a portion of the overall workload. Your 'unique' factor can benefit the company, and in return, the company pays you to do the job.

Where Is The Evidence of Your Skill Set?

Let's say that you are a sales student, and that's your 'it' factor. You want to land a job as the next sales assistant of a prestigious firm, and you want to convince your interviewer that you are capable to use your skills and make positive changes towards the future of the firm. But how do you prove that you have what it takes?

1 "Give Me An Example" – Interviewer

Your interviewer asks you to "sell this product" and hands you the new iPhoneX. In a quick improv, you have to think about why customers should be buying the new iPhoneX, why it is an obvious choice for anyone to purchase, and special qualities about the iPhoneX that makes it different from other phones.

Why take this option? Because you get to have the stage for approximately 30 seconds as you deliver the best sales pitch in your life to your interviewer. Interviewers will have the opportunity to see you in your element, which is sales and interacting with potential customers. They want to see how you operate under normal circumstances and the level of your skill set in your particular profession.

Why NOT to take this option? Because it's an improv performance, and the pressure of someone watching you can cause you to make mistakes, trip over your words, or say something that you didn't necessarily think over first. It's risky option, but if you do give a perfect improv sales pitch, you're placing yourself high on the list for the job.

2 "Here Is An Suggestion" – Self

You suggest a new marketing strategy to boost sales for a product/service that the company (you're applying to) is currently selling. This clearly shows that you are able to pitch new ideas during meetings and that you have ideas that can be useful to the company specifically.

Why take this option? Because you are in control of suggesting ideas and starting a conversation with your interviewer about why you proposed that suggestion. Through observation of how the company operates (if you have the chance to observe) and careful pre analysis of the company's different departments, individuals have the opportunity to take a consumer's stance and make suggestions.

Why NOT to take this option? Because there is a lot of pressure of what your suggestion can propose – it can be anything. You want your suggestion to be different from other applicants; if your interviewer responds to your suggestion with 'we get that a lot,' it means that someone else has already suggested the same thing. It's an unknown territory to trek in, and you never know how your interviewer will respond.

The Shoot-Your-Shot Elevator Pitch

In 30-60 seconds, try to summarize your profession and why an employer should consider you for a job. That is the elevator pitch. Perfecting an elevator pitch can push you up the corporate ladder from being an assistant to be a part of the leadership team of the company. Think about that paycheck increasing and increasing… okay now that's the reason why you should aim to nail an elevator pitch.

There's a reason why persuasive people are leaders. It's not just because they know how to climb the corporate ladder, but it's how they can talk their way up the ladder. Knowing how to talk, how to flatter others appropriately, and how to persuade others to give you opportunities (an exclusive interview with the CEO, contacts of important customers, and basically whatever you want) is the smartest way to get to the top of your industry.

Here's a hypothetical scenario: you just got in the elevator with the Human Resources executive of Richardson Media Management (RMM). With the few seconds that the both of you are standing together in the same elevator, your goal is to pitch yourself to get a job/position that you want. So, in the below scenario, Lisa Bonnet is trying to talk to the HR executive of a management company to work in their HR team.

Step 1: Introduce Yourself (Name and Background)

"Hi, my name is Lisa Bonnet and I am a HR major at the University of California-Berkeley."

Step 2: Compliment He/She or Their Company

General: "I've heard a lot about your company and the great things that RMM are currently doing."

Specific: "I read about the interview that you did with Forbes on the significance of the HR department in RMM… and I really agree with how social interactions can really determine the future of any company…"

Step 3: State Your Pitch (ease into it and don't be demanding)

"I'd be interested in applying for a position in the HR team."

Step 4: Ask Them A Question

"How can I schedule a meeting with you to discuss applying?"

Step 5: Wait For A Response

If the HR executive indicates that he/she is uninterested, they will say something along the lines of "Thank you, but we already have found a person for the job" or "I'm sorry, but we don't hire undergraduates," or "RMM is currently not accepting any more applications. I'd encourage you to apply elsewhere."

If the HR executive likes your pitch and wants to connect with you later, they will say something along the lines of "You can contact my assistant to schedule a meeting."

Step 6: Wrap Up The Pitch With A Conclusion

As you head out of the elevator, you can do one of the following depending on the response that you receive.

Your pitch got denied: "Well, thank you for your time and it was really lovely meeting you."

You pitch got accepted: "Thank you so much. I'll send an email to your assistant ASAP. I look forward to talking with you soon."

Asking Questions

At the end of an interview, the interviewer will ask "do you have any other questions for me?" You are likely to answer "Um, no thank you." And that will be the end of your interview.

Instead, you want to ask approximately two to three questions before you end an interview. Plan a few questions related to the company or school that you're applying to BEFORE an interview, so that you have a set of questions already prepared.

Asking questions can show that you're engaged and constantly pursuing any chance to learn more, which many employers find to be important qualities in their employees.

STEP FOUR: *Your Presentation Creates Impressions*

Individuals notice certain details when they first meet you, and it indirectly causes them to either have a positive or negative impression about you. This is why individuals should learn to maintain a visual presentation, from the way you dress down to the way you walk.

Tip 1

Be Aware of Your Surroundings

The way that you present yourself in social settings is a reflection of who you are. You want your reflection to be good – not getting drunk at a dinner party, for example – in case your future boss (or your current boss) is at the party as well. Or, in the digital era that we live in, a video of your less presentable self – such as getting in a fist fight – could easily be going around the media and happen to be in your boss's Facebook feed the next morning. Although it's a certain probability and it doesn't mean that you can never have fun again in your life after you land an important job, it does mean that you have to be more aware of your actions and the way that you uphold your social presence.

Always take into consideration about your location. Are you at a home party where it is just you and your close friends or are you at a pub on a St. Patrick's Day event or are you in a VIP exclusive club house surrounded by high profile individuals and A-listers? With a lingering warning sign at the back of your head telling you that you are in an appropriate and professional setting, that will help you determine the way that you should behave and act.

Tip 2

Dress For The Occasion

The occasion can be anything ranging from an office party to your day-to-day working outfit, but the point is to watch out for what is happening to dress appropriately for any event.

Learning how to dress is one thing. But learning how to make yourself stand out with your attire can be a tad more difficult to grasp. Not only do you have to dress to suit the occasion, it's important to understand your goal for a specific outfit.

In movies, you often hear the CEO of a company shout "who is that girl in the red dress last night that asked me for an interview?" before the main character appears on the screen. It's basically the same concept. If your goal is to stand out and make a lasting impression, make sure that you dress appropriately AND you add in a bit of extra thought to complete the look.

What do I mean by add in extra thought? For men, polish your leather shoes, iron out every possible crease in your suit, and learn to organize your hair. For women, you should pick an eye-catching color such as red for your dress or go an unexpected route with a suit, dress pants, and maybe some flats. Either way, you want to take the path that most individuals wouldn't dare trek, and THAT will be the element that makes you visually distinctive.

Furthermore, grooming and cleanliness are aspects that you need to be aware about. I can tell you the story about a tutor with an unpleasant odor about her that got her fired from teaching one of her students. Those tiny things that you may not notice can become a significant problem.

Acknowledging the minimalistic details about the way you act and present yourself can help you analyze how much change you need to implement.

Tip 3
Body Language
Good Posture – Confidence
Big Gestures – Confidence
Loud Voice – Confidence

The thing is that body language can tell someone everything they need to know about you. Without ever saying a word to you, it is possible that someone can 'figure you out' in a matter of seconds of observing you interact with others in a social setting.

Be aware of bad habits that you might have, including slouching shoulders or your voice trailing off before you finish a sentence. Eliminate those habits and try to adopt better ones that can make you a memorable individual in any setting.

7
Smash The System

I am sick of wearing suits and sticking to the old-fashioned rules, so how do I break the traditional system?

What happens if teenagers begin their own businesses?

It's an obvious answer: teenagers won't stick by the century-old rulebook. They have to take their own spin on young professionalism, and establish a brand-new culture fit for teenagers – not adults.

What We Think About *Business*

When you think about a business, you think about a man in his late 40s in a suit and tie at his desk reviewing files from a folder – taxes or some legal documents, either way it doesn't matter. Our common thought is that you have to be of a certain age to start a business, but in the 21st century, young adults and teenagers have started multimillion-dollar businesses through a wide range of technology resources and an increase in global interconnectivity.

A business can easily begin through launching a website, signing up for an Instagram business account, creating handmade products and selling them via Etsy, or conjuring an idea that is worthy of being made into a profitable service for clients. In a sense, getting started with a business and reaching potential clients can be simply done through your digital tablets.

On the flip side of the coin, there aren't many teenage entrepreneurs or teenage businesspeople. Our society is still so constricted in these profound ideologies about teenagers.

Map Out Your Own Rules

The plus side to owning your business and being the creator of your company is that you get to write the rules. As a teenager, I employ you to make a real difference – think about it – it's not every day that a teenager starts running a business. You didn't make a business to be like everyone else. You made a business so you could have the freedom to create whatever you like.

Ditch The Suit and Tie

You often get told that if you show up at an interview with baggy clothes and a hoodie, you won't get the job. Appearance and fashion sense are a must, unless you are applying for a job at Facebook.

The most common advice for interview-wear is casual smart and professional attire. But here's the thing: teenagers are not supposed to be constricted. In a teenager-run business and workplace, it's supposed to be fun and different. As soon as you open up your business and start hiring, stop following all the rules about how you should dress and show up at an interview.

You are young, so you have the right to LOOK young.

Encourage your employers to wear something that best represents themselves. I don't mean to say, "take out that Miami bikini from the closet that you've been dying to wear." I'm saying that your own fashion sense has to be specific to you, and it has to be something that makes you feel professional without society's lingering suit-and-tie stereotype.

Young employees should not be pressured to wear the common 'professional attire' and young entrepreneurs should be the ones that are paving the future for a less traditional working culture. Overall, your employees are a reflection of your company inside out, and each business should always have a specific style (Facebook is t-shirt and jeans!). Your visual representation is a clear illustration of the message that you want to send to your clients, partners, online following, and visitors of your business workplace.

Depending on your industry, you may or may not want to consider the below ideas when it comes to acknowledging your company style and what the majority of your employees are wearing. It can definitely set the atmosphere of the entire workplace.

1) Have an OOTDay or OOTWeek or OOTMonth to highlight the best dressed employee if your brand is focused on fashion!
2) If you are a creative retail shop, encourage your employees to dress around and not be afraid to express themselves through their outfit!
3) Have a shoe-customization contest for your employees on special occasions if you are a footwear company!
4) Have a competition between your chefs to create a brand-new vegan dish that will be on the menu if you are a vegan-focused restaurant!

Young Professionalism *Culture*

This is a whole new concept with zero range but an incredible potential – think about a teenage CEO graduating high school early, running their own business, managing their own team of young professionals, pitching to potential clients through social events, and establishing a workplace culture with a majority of employees that are under 18.

And yes, you're thinking about all the possible ways that this could go wrong.

To better articulate your concerns, I've drawn out two likely scenarios for you here: 1) If the teenage CEO borrowed money from the bank or a group of investors for his/her business and can't pay them back, will parents get involved? and 2) If the teenage CEO cannot control a group of young adult employees due to lack of respect or lack of order, how will he/she control the chaos?

Once again, these concerns have fallen under the influence of teenage stereotypes. Think about it: a teenager that has the will and the ability to create a business under the age of 18 is already ten times more competent in a working environment compared to the rest of us. Anyone that have started their own business has put in a tremendous amount of work and countless hours of time – and to have that dedication for something means that teenagers can be able to be professional and mature.

Like any other businessperson in this industry, every CEO needs a vice CEO, or better yet – a group of advisors. Being the entrepreneur, founder, or creator of your own company does not mean that you have what it takes to maintain your company's survival as it encounters a competitive market. Listening to all angles of advice and implementing good advice will benefit the future of your company.

As your company grows and your customers increase, every teenage entrepreneur needs to understand to divide the workload and start hiring. Reaching out to other working teenagers or interviewing young adults that want a chance to work can help you is the first step to establishing a young professionalism working culture. You can't have a 'young professional' culture without hiring young professionals.

Where Do I Find Young Professionals?

Teenagers and young adults can't afford to move to a new location or fly halfway across the world just for the sake of a new job. So instead, begin setting up online job openings on your main company website, other hiring websites, or via social media. Go to your local newspaper or local magazine and set up a job opening ad for your company. You want to start by contacting potential individuals for certain jobs if you are well-connected or you have mutual connections.

Finding dependable and professional young adults can be difficult, which is why every teenage CEO needs to be able to effectively analyze every potential employee. Will this person cause trouble? Will this person handle the job seriously? Will this person follow company guidelines? Will this person go above and beyond the standards for this job?

As the person that is possibly sitting at every interview and asking questions (unless you have a hiring manager), you have to remember that every person that you hire will be a part of the foundation of your company.

NOTE: since you are under 18, you will need at least one trusted adult at the side to help you deal with legal purposes.

What can your trusted adult do?

1) Find you a business lawyer/agent, who can help you launch your business officially.

2) Help you set up an official bank account, a PayPal or Payoneer account, tax info, or manage your transactions.

3) Talk to adult clients for you, if needed.

4) Get firsthand advice and information (be sure to ask multiple people to gain different perspectives and insight into a problem or situation).

How To Kick Start Your Company In The First Few Months?

The first few months will be no doubt be a tough cookie.

A teenage CEO will have to ensure that every aspect of the business is running smoothly. For example, your sales department is in search of new clients and marketplaces to sell your product/service; your marketing department is finding new strategies to promote your product/service; your productions department is in charge of overseeing product/service quality; your administration department is establishing daily business operations.

Even though every department might start off with only one or two people, you still need to have high expectations for every employee. Keeping track of every employee and every department's progress is essential to kickstarting your business off the ground.

How To Deal With The 'Age' Thing Between CEO and Employees?

The truth is that everyone could be of the same age range, which causes problems. Since not every employee will be on the same page when it comes to their maturity level and being professional, a teenage CEO needs to display assertive authority in order to gain the respect of his/her employees. You want your employees to take you seriously, so that they don't slack off at their job or not listen to you in an important meeting.

How To Interact With Adult Clients

Will you be rejected a collaboration, a project, a funding, or a business deal because of your age? That's a likely yes.

You will lose customers because of your age, because a majority of adults are hesitant to trust in a product/service that may not be reliable or is made by a group of teenagers. My advice is to do your best to convince customers of your company's professional stance, but if your customers will not budge, leave it be. The same goes for any business relationship.

Throughout your business journey, you will have to narrow down a loyal target audience. It could be teenagers or adults or a blend of both. Your audience should be people that provide honest feedback and enthusiasm for your business, but never dubious of the quality of your product/service because of your age. You want the phrase of "that underaged group of teenagers behind the entire operation" to be placed in a positive context as opposed to a negative one.

To summarize, the customers that really enjoy and appreciate your company's product/service will be a part of a loyal audience that wouldn't give a damn about a thing called age.

How To Establish Culture

Establishing workplace culture can include the atmosphere of the location, the diversity of the employees, the behavior of the employees, and the interaction between people.

Let's say that your company is a fashion retail boutique targeted at young women and located in a second-floor warehouse with good lighting. Your employees are predominantly 20 to 30-something females; their attire branches from bright yellow blazers to sundresses.

In this company, their established culture has been focused on the importance of communication. All employees are exchanging work-related conversation about things like package delays and the newly launched line as they walk between the small wooden desks. This example of workplace culture is open and positive, which allows for higher productivity amongst everyone.

If your company is a place where people DON'T want to go to work, it will establish a pessimistic culture and an exhausting environment for employees to be in. Your job as the CEO is to encourage positive workplace culture – your leadership will also be an important aspect that will influence the overall workplace culture of your company.

8
Stereotyping

I'm constantly getting rejected by employers because of my age, how do I change that?

I read something a few months ago while scrolling on Stack Exchange when I encountered a teenager asking for advice on how to freelance. This was the response that he/she received from another user:

"

I realize you may have a wide range of skills and may feel you are very adept at some things, but there's no possible way a 16 or 17-year-old can have even 2 years of accurate, real-world, experience. Let alone someone younger. I don't wish to offend you, but you don't know regardless of how capable or talented you think you are. Situations and complications arise in technical projects which can only be overcome through experience.

"

I want to highlight the point about EXPERIENCE.

In some cases, it's true that your level of knowledge cannot overcome the amount of experience. But as a teenager who's trying to get your first job, your strengths are your dedication and hard-working attitude towards this job. An employer always wants to see someone that has those qualities and is passionate about their company.

Employers reject teenagers for so many reasons aside from the minor age of employment: lack of real-world experience, don't know how to handle a crisis, don't know how to overcome obstacles, lack of maturity, etc. Your job is to PROVE THEM WRONG. You do not want your abilities and your personality to be regarded and categorized into the common teenager stereotype.

1
Lack of Maturity

Yes, teenagers can joke around and have fun. That doesn't mean that their age can determine how they will act in a given workplace scenario.

You often get told that you have to pass the whole 'high school' thing before you can start working, and then after that, you'll finally be considered mature enough to start working. This is why a majority of companies reject high school students that are applying for jobs, because they're afraid that their lack of maturity will cause them to not focus on the job.

Employers turn their heads away from the possibility of hiring teenagers when they can be hiring adults… they believe that hiring teenagers will be a useless investment, because teenagers might get bored after one hour into the job and start scrolling on their phones.

But the truth is that not all teenagers are lazy and undedicated, some are extremely hard working and can take their job very seriously. Yet, employers put all teenagers under one category for their judgement – a group of people that they claim to be too immature amongst other things.

The only way to turn this stereotype around is to prove that you are not lazy, not undedicated, and not scrolling on your phone during your shift. You have to prove that you are focused on your job and you are putting in the work, so your employer can have a bit more trust in the next teenager that they hire.

2
Lack of Experience

As a 16-year-old, what specialty can you have? What other work experiences can you have? What would make people pick you over some 22-year-old that graduated with a degree from some community college when you are only a high schooler? It always comes down to a tough interview question about a teenager's lack of experience.

Although you can't simply make up a list of experiences on your resume, you can make the most of what you have already done in high school, extracurriculars, summer internships, freelancing jobs, etc. Don't dodge the question, but make up for what you lack (which is experience) with what you already have. Talk about how you are a fast learner and emphasize on your work ethic. The main point is to pitch yourself and give every job opportunity your best shot.

Your level of experience will not be able to match up to a 22-year-old's, but you have time – time to gain more experience, time to inquire about every job opening, and time to work your ass off until you find yourself a job.

3
Lack of Knowledge

Since teenagers are still technically in school, employers may think that a teenager does not have the level of knowledge to pass the basic threshold for a company or for a specific job. Why? Because of being IN SCHOOL.

Employers quickly assume that teenagers cannot meet the requirements for a job, because they think that there are still things that teenagers do not know or has not learned yet. Traditional thinkers believe that only people that are older can have the brain capacity to understand a certain topic or master a certain skill.

Yet, teenagers have the same brain capacity, from doing a basic job to running a multi-million-dollar business corporation – think about all the teenage entrepreneurs with a hefty net worth.

Lack of Motivation

The common stereotype for teenagers is lack of motivation and laziness. The core reason why teenagers are lazy is because they don't have an INCENTIVE to work. A stay-at-home single mom with three kids is forced to do anything she can to support her family, so she starts two blogs and accept any freelance job opportunity. An incentive will drive you to do anything that you want to do, but only if you have a reason to do it.

While there is a handful of teenagers that are unmotivated and lazy, there are still teenagers who work hard and have ambition. Employers need to take the chance to determine the best candidate for a job, and it may as well be a teenager with self-motivation and true dedication.

Afternote
Just one last thing.

1% of people succeed… the other 99% are still squandering hopelessly in the midst of their confusing adolescence. Too many teenagers seek comfort in the paths of alcohol, midnight Twitter feuds, college hookup culture, etc. As an alternative, many don't choose to fight for an ambitious pursuit towards their future. Thinking about the future is stressful – it's time-consuming to plan out your goals and actually do the work to meet those goals.

Understand this: "The countless hours you spend on these so-called 'distractions' can continue to build up for days, weeks, months, and even years." It's important to snap out of your comfort zone and face reality, because you don't get to be a teenager for very long. Don't become a retired 65-year-old that spent the entirety of his life in the same office, working for the same lame boss, and receiving a steady paycheck. Don't be the one that regrets not starting a business when you could – your opportunity is now, so seize it.

I'll see you soon

—

Shirley Martin Wang

Acknowledgments

I want to thank a few people.

I want to thank a few people.

    My editor Sabrina for her dedication to editing this book and being supportive. I could not have been able to survive those last weeks of publishing and finishing this book if it was not for your encouragement. I would not have asked anyone else to edit this book, because your incredible editing skill into any form of publication is absolutely impeccable (I'm not biased). A lot of people say that we are polar opposites – that you're patient and thorough while I'm spontaneous and perhaps rash – but I think that's the reason why we somehow work really well together.

    My sister Sharon for always being available as the shoulder for me cry on, an ear to listen to my complaints, and always enduring my stupid life choices. Every human needs a best friend. I'm so glad I found mine before I could spell S-H-I-R-L-E-Y.

    A shout-out to Philip Hartmann for being Philip Hartmann and spamming me with Kayla content – I don't say this to your face, but I really admire you for your maturity and the way you don't exaggerate or overcomplicate things.

    To Rafaela for her unquantifiable support system 24/7 and being the best of friends even though we are separated by an ocean (or sea?).

    Sandy for being my cover photographer as well as a joy to be around and talk to. Two years later, we should apply for Harvard just for the fun of it.

    Bonny for worrying about my health due to yearbook.

Mulayne for being my go-to DG gal – you give the best relationship advice.

Richard! Thank you tremendously for your insight into the business industry and giving me some honest suggestions for my book – it definitely made me come to my senses and realize that I had to take it one step at a time.

Meghan – hello – you're probably surprised that you're in here. If you see this, then I have to say that I'm very proud of you for making it this far into a book that's not filled with juicy drama and gossip.

Also, I want to thank the people that agreed to do interviews and were more than willing to share their incredible entrepreneurship stories. Paola Ochoa, Beatrice aka The Bliss Bean, Hedy Zhou, Ellie Everett, Tricia Panlaqui, Brennan Agranoff, and Jade Darmawangsa.

I was so immensely thankful that each and every one of you took the time out of your schedules to answer those interview questions, shoot a quick video response, or even did a virtual interview with me. I'm so inspired by the great things that each of you are accomplishing in your own fields, and especially the hard work that you dedicate into your work. I hope your stories inspire more teenagers to start their own business, create their first YouTube channel, and most of all – pursue their dreams.

All in all, I'm so grateful to every last person that congratulated me on my first book or was even merely curious about what the hell I was even doing.

Lastly – to my family. My dad for not knowing everything about what I'm doing all the time, but an all-time hilarious soul. My brother as he is my favorite person in the world. And to my mother for the insane amount of time that she devotes to spontaneously teaching me about business, for forcing me to read books, and for never telling me that my writing career could be a total flop unless I was J.K Rowling.

About The Author
Shirley Martin Wang

Shirley Martin Wang is the 15-year-old author of Business Insider with a Teenager.

She is Taiwanese but has lived in China her entire life. Currently, she is in her sophomore year of high school at the American International School of Guangzhou.

A bit of background.
Shirley began writing mystery and adventure novels at the age of eight. She has continued to write in multiple genres for the last seven years. In her freshman year of high school, from her passion for photography, she created her portrait photography business based in China. Shirley also dabbled in YouTube and videography, which later landed her local gigs shooting promotional videos and advertisements.

After realizing that all the books in the Leadership, Management, and Business genre were targeted at adults, Shirley came up with the idea of a business book for teenagers.

She finished writing Business Insider with a Teenager in less than a month during her quarantine period (due to the COVID-19 outbreak) and self-published it on multiple platforms.

In addition to writing, she is also a portrait photography business owner, a freelance videographer, an online coach for Teen Biz Insider, and a journalist/columnist at her local magazine.

Connect With Her

Send her a message via Instagram @itshirleyz
All Inquiries: shirleytbusiness@gmail.com

www.ingramcontent.com/pod-product-compliance
Lightning Source LLC
Chambersburg PA
CBHW050012230526
45465CB00003BB/1383